FANSHAWE COLLEGE
E. S. L.
RESOURCE CENTRE

S0-AXL-943

76

GRAMMAR DIMENSIONS 1
PLATINUM EDITION

WORKBOOK

Cheryl Benz

Miami-Dade Community College

HH **Heinle & Heinle**
Thomson Learning

Australia Canada Denmark Japan Mexico New Zealand
Philippines Puerto Rico Singapore Spain United Kingdom United States

Acquisitions Editor: Eric Bredenberg
Senior Developmental Editor: Amy Lawler
Production Editor: Michael Burggren
Senior Marketing Manager: Charlotte Sturdy
Manufacturing Coordinator: MaryBeth Hennebury
Composition: The Clarinda Company
Project Management: Emily Autumn
Cover Design: Hannus Design Associates

Photos on pages 1 and 47, courtesy of Pat Martin.

Copyright © 2000 Heinle & Heinle, a division of Thomson Learning, Inc.
Thomson Learning$_{TM}$ is a registered trademark used herein under license.

All rights reserved. No part of this work covered by the copyright hereon may be reproduced or used in any form or by any means—graphic, electronic, or mechanical, including photocopying, recording, taping, or information storage and retrieval systems—without the written permission of the publisher.

For permission to use material from this text, contact us:
web   www.thomsonrights.com
fax   1-800-730-2215
phone   1-800-730-2214

Heinle & Heinle Publishers
20 Park Plaza
Boston, MA 02116

UK/EUROPE/MIDDLE EAST:
Thomson Learning
Berkshire House
168-173 High Holborn
London, WC1 V 7AA, United Kingdom

AUSTRALIA/NEW ZEALAND:
Nelson/Thomson Learning
102 Dodds Street
South Melbourne
Victoria 3205 Australia

CANADA:
Nelson/Thomson Learning
1120 Birchmount Road
Scarborough, Ontario
Canada M1K 5G4

LATIN AMERICA:
Thomson Learning
Seneca, 53
Colonia Polanco
11560 México D.F. México

ASIA (excluding Japan):
Thomson Learning
60 Albert Street #15-01
Albert Complex
Singapore 189969

JAPAN:
Thomson Learning
Palaceside Building, 5F
1-1-1 Hitotsubashi, Chiyoda-ku
Tokyo 100 0003, Japan

SPAIN:
Thomson Learning
Calle Magallanes, 25
28015-Madrid
Espana

ISBN: 0-8384-0266-6

This book is printed on acid-free recycled paper.

Printed in the United States of America
2 3 4 5 6 7 8 9 04 03 02 01 00

TOEFL® is a registered trademark of Educational Testing Service (ETS). This product is not endorsed or approved by ETS.

CONTENTS

THE VERB BE

Affirmative Statements, Subject Pronouns

▶ **EXERCISE 1**   *(Focus 1, page 2)*

My name is Juan.
I'm from Mexico.
I am 19.
I'm single.
I'm a student.

I'm Julia.
I'm German.
I'm 19.
I'm single.
I'm a student.

My name is Rosa.
I'm Puerto Rican.
I'm 35 years old.
I'm divorced.
I am a teacher.

I'm Yumiko
I'm from Japan.
I'm 35.
I'm married.
I'm an engineer.

Put the sentence in the correct order.

▶ **EXAMPLE:** are/ Juan and Rosa/ Hispanic. <u>Juan and Rosa are Hispanic.</u>

1. divorced. / is / Rosa _____

2. Yumiko / Japanese. / is _____

3. are / single. / Juan and Julia _____

4. 35. / The engineer / is _____

5. is / The German / a student. _____

6. from Puerto Rico. / The teacher / is _____

7. Juan and Julia / 19 years old. / are _____

8. a student. / is / The Mexican _____

9. Asian. / Yumiko / is _____

10. are / single. / The students _____

▶ **EXERCISE 2**   *(Focus 1, page 2)*

Fill in the blanks with *is* or *are*.

▶ **EXAMPLE:** The students _____*are*_____ 19 years old.

1. Yumiko _____ Japanese.

2. Rosa _____ a teacher.

3. The engineer _____ Japanese.

4. Yumiko and Rosa _____ 35.

5. The students _____ 19 years old.

▶ **EXERCISE 3**   *(Focus 2, page 4)*

Replace the noun phrase with a subject pronoun.

▶ **EXAMPLE:** Julia is German. _____*She*_____ is a student.

1. Julia is from Europe. _____ is German.

2. Juan and Julia are 19 years old. _____ are single.

3. Rosa is from Puerto Rico. _____ is a teacher.

4. The student is 19 years old. _____ is Mexican.

5. Japan is a country. _____ is in Asia.

6. My name is Yumiko. _____ am Japanese.

7. You and I are from Asia. _____ are Asians.

8. Mexico is a country. _____ is in North America.

9. Juan is from Mexico. _____ is single.

10. Rosa is a teacher. _____ is divorced.

Write three sentences about yourself using *be*. Then write three sentences about a partner.

► EXAMPLE: I am from Brazil.

YOU

1. _____

_____

2. _____

_____

3. _____

_____

PARTNER

1. _____

_____

2. _____

_____

3. _____

_____

► **EXERCISE 5**   *(Focus 3, page 7)*

Rewrite the sentence using contractions (subject pronoun + *be*).

► EXAMPLE: Juan is Hispanic. He's Hispanic. _____

1. Julia and Juan are single. _____

2. Julia is a student. _____

3. Rosa is from Puerto Rico. _____

4. Yumiko is an engineer from Japan. _____

5. Mexico and the United States are in North America. _____

6. My name is Julia. I am European. _____

7. Julia and I are students. _____

8. Julia and Rosa are single. _____

9. Yumiko is 35 years old. _____

10. Juan is a student from Mexico. _____

▶ **EXERCISE 6**   *(Focus 4, page 9)*

1. Ask your partner the following questions:
   a. What's your name?
   b. Where are you from?
   c. How are you?
2. Introduce your partner to the other people in your class.

▶ **EXERCISE 7**   *(Focus 4, page 9)*

Think about the correct way to greet the people listed below. Write *formal* if the greeting should be formal. Write *informal* if the greeting can be informal. Act out the greetings with a partner.

   1. your teacher _____

   2. your mother _____

   3. a classmate _____

   4. a young child _____

   5. a doctor _____

   6. a police officer _____

THE VERB BE

Yes/No Questions, Be + Adjective, Negative Statements

▶ **EXERCISE 1**   *(Focus 1, page 16)*

Fill in the blanks below. Then choose the correct answer to the puzzles.

GUESS THE PLACE	GUESS WHO I AM
_____ this place in Europe?	Am I female?
Yes, _____ _____ .	No, _____ _____.
_____ _____ in Russia?	_____ _____ an actor?
No, _____ _____ .	_____ , you aren't.
_____ _____ in France?	_____ _____ a singer?
_____ , it is.	No, _____ _____.
_____ _____ a museum?	_____ _____ an athlete?
Yes, _____ _____.	_____ , you are.
_____ _____ in Paris?	_____ _____ a soccer player?
Yes, _____ _____.	Yes, _____ _____.
Is it _____?	_____ _____ from Brazil?
(the Hermitage, the Louvre)	Yes, you are.
	Am I _____?
	(Pele, Michael Jordan)

GUESS WHO WE ARE

Are we girls?

_____, you aren't.

_____ _____ from the United States?

No, _____ _____.

_____ _____ from Great Britain?

Yes, _____ _____.

_____ _____ part of the royal family?

_____, you are.

Are we _____?

(Prince William and Prince Harry, Ted and John Kennedy)

▶ **EXERCISE 2** *(Focus 1, page 16)*

Imagine that you are a famous person. Your partner must guess who you are by asking Yes or No questions.

▶ **EXAMPLE:** **A:** *Are you an actress?*
B: *Yes, I am.*
A: *Are you an American?*
B: *No, I'm not . . .*

▶ **EXERCISE 3** *(Focus 2, page 18)*

busy	good	sick	healthy	ugly	young
angry	energetic	funny	overweight	strong	tall
happy	beautiful	poor	serious	weak	sad
thin	messy	rich	intelligent	loud	noisy
athletic	frightened	shy	outgoing	quiet	tired
organized	interesting	short	talkative	neat	calm
nervous	homesick	handsome	friendly	lonely	old

PART A

Write five sentences describing yourself. Use the list of adjectives on page 6 to help you.

▶ EXAMPLE: _I am outgoing._

1. _____

2. _____

3. _____

4. _____

5. _____

PART B

Using the same list, write five sentences about your parents.

▶ EXAMPLE: _My parents are happy._

1. _____

2. _____

3. _____

4. _____

5. _____

PART C

Using the same list, write five sentences about someone else in your family.

▶ EXAMPLE: _My uncle is athletic._

1. _____

2. _____

3. _____

4. _____

5. _____

▶ **EXERCISE 4**   *(Focuses 1 and 2, page 16 and page 18)*

Share with a partner some of the sentences you wrote in Exercise 3. Ask Yes or No questions about the people your partner describes.

▶ **EXAMPLE:** **A:** *My uncle is athletic.*

   B: *Is he a basketball player?*

   A: *No he isn't; he is a tennis player.*

▶ **EXERCISE 5**   *(Focus 3, page 22)*

Using the list of adjectives from Exercise 3, write five *negative* statements about yourself. Share the statements with your partner.

▶ **EXAMPLE:**   I am not neat.
_____

   1. _____

   2. _____

   3. _____

   4. _____

   5. _____

▶ **EXERCISE 6**   *(Focus 3, page 22)*

Write sentences describing the pictures, using the cues and negative statements. Follow the example.

▶ **EXAMPLE:** tall building / short <u>The building isn't short. It's tall.</u>

1. big mouse / small _____

_____

2. boring speaker / interesting _____

_____

3. crying baby / quiet _____

_____

4. fat Santa / thin _____

_____

5. young woman / old _____

_____

6. handsome man / ugly _____

_____

7. soft toy / hard _____

_____

8. busy bees / lazy _____

_____

9. easy problem / difficult _____

_____

10. tired children / awake _____

_____

UNIT 3

THE VERB BE

Wh-Question Words, Prepositions of Location

Complete the story by filling in each blank with the correct question word and the form of *be*. The first one has been done for you as an example.

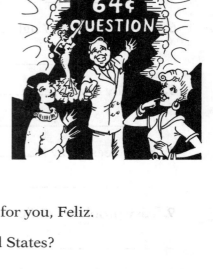

Monte: Welcome to the "64-Cent Question," the game show where we ask easy questions and the contestants can win up to 64 cents. I'm your host Monte Money, and our two contestants tonight are Feliz Happy and Sandy Beach.

Monte: _____How are_____ you tonight, Feliz?

Feliz: I'm just happy to be here, Monte.

Monte: Great, and _____ _____ you, Sandy?

Sandy: Fine, thank you, Monte.

Monte: Great, now let's begin tonight's game. The first question is for you, Feliz.

_____ _____ the capital of the United States?

Feliz: Washington, D.C.

Monte: Right! Now, for you Sandy. _____ _____ the director of the movie *ET?*

Sandy: Steven Spielberg.

Monte: Great! Now Feliz, _____ _____ plants green?

Feliz: Because they contain chlorophyll.

Monte: You've got it. Sandy, _____ _____ _____ the pyramids in Egypt?

Sandy: About 4,700 years old.

Monte: Correct! Feliz, _____ _____ the first day of spring?

Feliz: March 21.

Monte: Right again! Now, Sandy. _____ _____ Leonardo da Vinci's painting commonly called the *Mona Lisa?*

Sandy: In the Louvre in Paris.

Monte: Yes! For you, Feliz, _____ _____ _____ seven times eight?

Feliz: Fifty-six.

Monte: You're right again. Sandy, _____ _____ the author of *Tom Sawyer?*

Sandy: Mark Twain.

Monte: Okay. Feliz, _____ _____ the Statue of Liberty located?

Feliz: In New York.

Monte: Finally, for you, Sandy, the last question. _____ _____ Thanksgiving celebrated in the United States?

Sandy: On the fourth Thursday in November.

Monte: Amazing, folks! We have a tie! Well, tune in next week for the "64-Cent Question!"

▶ **EXERCISE 2**   *(Focus 2, page 33)*

This is an information gap activity. **With a partner, take turns asking each other word meanings. One of you covers up the answers in Part A and asks the partner for meanings and sample sentences for the five words. The answers are in Part B. Then change, using the words in Part B whose answers you covered in Part A.**

PART A

1. banjo _____

_____

2. talkative _____

_____

3. lumberjack _____

_____

4. fog _____

_____

5. sailor _____

_____

1. hail (noun) hard round pieces of frozen rain—The hail destroyed the plants.

2. pretend (verb) to imagine; to make believe—I like to pretend I'm a clown.

3. ignore (verb) to pay no attention to—He ignores his mother when she tells him to clean his room.

4. chubby (adjective) round and fat—The little boy had a chubby face.

5. dye (verb) to change the color—She dyes her hair.

PART B

1. hail

2. pretend

3. ignore

4. chubby

5. dye

1. banjo (noun) a musical instrument with a round body and five strings—The musician played her banjo.

2. talkative (adjective) talking a lot—That talkative woman doesn't let anyone else say a word.

3. lumberjack (noun) a person who cuts down trees—The lumberjack cut down the giant tree.

4. fog (noun) clouds that reach to the ground—I could hardly see through the fog.

5. sailor (noun) a person who works on a boat or ship—The sailor turned the ship into the wind.

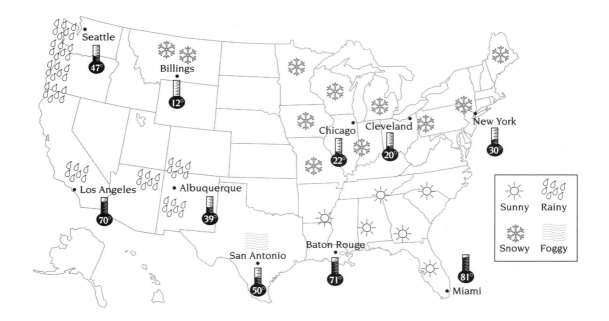

Sunny   Rainy

Snowy   Foggy

▶ **EXERCISE 3**   *(Focus 3, page 33)*

Answer the questions using the information on the map.

1. How's the weather in Miami today? _____

_____

2. What's the temperature in Chicago? _____

_____

3. How's the weather in Seattle? _____

_____

4. What's the temperature in New York? _____

_____

5. How's the weather in Los Angeles? _____

_____

6. How's the weather in San Antonio? _____

_____

7. What's the temperature in Cleveland? _____

_____

8. How's the weather in Billings? _____

_____

9. How's the weather in Albuquerque? _____

_____

10. What's the temperature in Baton Rogue? _____

_____

▶ **EXERCISE 4**   *(Focus 3, page 33)*

Find the weather map in today's newspaper. Take turns asking your partner questions about the weather in different U.S. cities.

▶ **EXERCISE 5**   *(Focus 4, page 35)*

Look at this map of the time zones of Europe and answer the questions on the next page.

1. It's 7 A.M. in London. What time is it in Paris? _____

2. It's 9 A.M. in Lisbon. What time is it in Berlin? _____

3. It's 11 A.M. in Rome. What time is it in Madrid? _____

4. It's 10 A.M. in Dublin. What time is it in Amsterdam? _____

5. It's 11 A.M. in London. What time is it in Rome? _____

Write five more questions using this pattern. Ask your partner for the answers.

1. _____

_____

2. _____

_____

3. _____

_____

4. _____

_____

5. _____

_____

_____

Draw the shapes according to the directions below. The first two steps have already been drawn. Write a sentence about each figure using the verb *to be* and a prepositional phrase. The first one has been done for you as an example.

1. Draw a square.

2. Draw a triangle above the square.

3. Draw two rectangles under the square.

4. Draw a face on the square.

5. Draw a circle behind the square.

1. <u>The square is under the triangle.</u>
   _____

2. _____
   _____

3. _____
   _____

4. _____
   _____

5. _____
   _____

1. Draw a circle.

1. _____

_____

2. Draw another circle next to the first circle.

2. _____

_____

3. Draw a line between the circles.

3. _____

_____

4. Draw a square in the circles.

4. _____

_____

5. Draw two triangles opposite each circle.

5. _____

_____

1. Draw a man.

1. _____

_____

2. Draw a woman near the man.

2. _____

_____

3. Draw a boy in front of the man.

3. _____

_____

4. Draw a girl between the man and the woman.

4. _____

_____

5. Draw a house behind the people.

5. _____

_____

Draw a simple picture, but don't show it to your partner. Tell your partner how to draw the picture using the verb *to be* and a prepositional phrase and then compare the two pictures.

Using *where are* or *where is*, write a question about the location of each cue word. Then answer your questions with the help of the picture. Follow the example.

► **EXAMPLE:** towels _Where are the towels? On the dresser._

1. keys _____

_____

2. shirt _____

_____

3. pants _____

_____

4. books _____

_____

5. shoes _____

_____

6. sweater _____

_____

7. jewelry _____

_____

8. glasses _____

_____

9. pillow _____

_____

10. brush _____

_____

EXERCISES FOR THE TOEFL® TEST

Units 1–3

Choose the *one* word or phrase that best completes each sentence.

1. The students _____ from Mexico.
   (A) and
   (B) be
   (C) are
   (D) is

2. When _____?
   (A) time is it
   (B) is your vacation
   (C) is Canada
   (D) old are you

3. _____ is married.
   (A) They
   (B) It
   (C) We
   (D) She

4. _____ students in level 1.
   (A) She is
   (B) It is
   (C) They are
   (D) I am

5. _____? It means very big.
   (A) What means huge
   (B) What is the spelling of huge
   (C) What is the meaning of huge
   (D) What is the pronunciation of huge

6. _____ shy and athletic.
   (A) She's
   (B) It isn't
   (C) Am
   (D) It's

7. The student _____ Japanese.
   (A) is
   (B) am
   (C) be
   (D) she

8. _____ an English teacher.
   (A) They are
   (B) I'm
   (C) They're
   (D) To be

9. _____ Montreal? _____ in Quebec.

    (A) Where is . . . It's   (C) Where is . . . Is

    (B) Where be . . . It is   (D) When is . . . It's

10. Dr. Martin is _____ .

    (A) opens   (C) school

    (B) busy   (D) yes

11. You _____ short.

    (A) it's   (C) no

    (B) am   (D) aren't

12. _____ ? I'm 35.

    (A) How age are you   (C) How old you are

    (B) How are you   (D) How old are you

13. _____ am not short.

    (A) I   (C) You

    (B) We're   (D) I'm

14. A: Hi! I'm Anne Parker.

    B: _____ .

    (A) Nice to you meet,   (C) Is nice, Anne.

        Ms. Parker   (D) Nice to meet you, Anne.

    (B) Nice to meet you, Ms. Anne

15. _____ your teacher?

    (A) Who   (C) Who's

    (B) Who are   (D) Whose

Identify the _one_ underlined word or phrase that must be changed for the sentence to be grammatically correct.

16. Is it cold? What's the temperature today? It has 30 degrees.
     A   B   C   D

17. Is Jose from China? No, Jose's no from China.
     A   B   C   D

18. Tense I am? Yes, you are; try to relax.
     A   B   C   D

19. Who is your teacher? Ms. Betty is my teacher.
     A   B   C   D

20. How are those problems? He isn't difficult.
     A   B   C   D

21. Are you single? Yes, I'm.
     A   B   C   D

22. Is it raining? No, is not. It's sunny.
     A   B   C   D

23. <u>What time</u> <u>it is</u>? <u>It's three o'clock</u> <u>in the afternoon</u>.
      A   **B**   **C**   **D**

24. <u>How's</u> <u>the weather today</u>? <u>Is</u> <u>cool and rainy</u>.
      A   **B**   **C** **D**

25. <u>When</u> <u>are you wet</u>? <u>I'm wet</u> because of <u>the rain</u>.
      A   **B**   **C**   **D**

NOUNS

Count and Noncount Nouns, *Be* + Adjective + Noun

▶ **EXERCISE 1**   *(Focus 1, page 48)*

Look at the underlined nouns and circle all noncount nouns. The first one has been done for you as an example.

(Chicken) is a kind of <u>meat</u>.
<u>Chickens</u> are birds with <u>wings</u> and <u>feathers</u>.

1. Is there <u>money</u> in the <u>jar</u>?
2. Yes, there is some <u>change</u>.
3. Is there a <u>quarter</u> in the jar?
4. No, but I think there are two <u>dimes</u> and a <u>nickel</u>.

5. His <u>clothing</u> is old.
6. His <u>pants</u> are torn.
7. His <u>shirt</u> is dirty.

▶ **EXERCISE 2** *(Focus 2, page 49)*

Put each word below in its correct category. Write *a* or *an* in front of each word.

tie	month	potato	blouse	helicopter
day	carrot	airplane	radish	undershirt
pea	sweater	truck	uniform	automobile
herb	year	week	train	hour

CLOTHES	TRANSPORTATION	VEGETABLES	TIME
1.	1.	1.	1.
2.	2.	2.	2.
3.	3.	3.	3.
4.	4.	4.	4.
5.	5.	5.	5.

▶ **EXERCISE 3** *(Focus 3, page 52)*

Complete the story by filling in each blank with the correct plural form of each word below. The first letter of each word is given to help you. The first one has been done for you as an example.

princess	toy	witch	monster	candy	hero
girl	class	bat	country	holiday	knife
cat	party	door	baby	ax	orange
fairy	story	wish	treat	boy	trick
house					

Halloween in the United States

It is interesting to learn about <u>holidays</u> in different c_____. Halloween is celebrated on October 31 in the United States. Small children and even b_____ wear costumes. Some children like frightening costumes. They dress like w_____ and m_____. The scary costumes can include plastic k_____ and a_____ with fake blood, but their weapons don't really hurt anyone. Some b_____ dress like Superman and Batman and other h_____. F_____ that grant people w_____ or Cinderella and Sleeping Beauty and other p_____ from s_____ are popular costumes for g_____. Other children dress like c_____, b_____, and other animals. In the afternoon, the children have p_____ in their c_____ at school. When it gets dark, the children knock on all the d_____ of the h_____ in their neighborhood. The people in the houses give the children t_____ like c_____, o_____ and other fruit, and small t_____. If they don't receive treats, some children play t_____.

▶ **EXERCISE 4** *(Focus 4, page 54)*

Listen to your teacher read the regular plural nouns you used in Exercise 3. Write each word in the correct category according to its pronunciation. The first one has been done for you as an example.

/z/	/s/	/iz/
holidays		

▶ **EXERCISE 5** *(Focus 4, page 54)*

Practice saying each of the words in the lists you made in Exercise 4. Use a tape recorder if possible to check your pronunciation.

Write the irregular plural form of each of the following nouns in the correct category. Use a dictionary to look up words you do not know how to spell. The first one has been done for you as an example.

Nouns

man	fish	child	person
woman	ox	sheep	foot
deer	goose	hoof	moose
tooth	mouse	hair	

HUMANS	ANIMALS	BODY PARTS
people		

Circle the mistakes in count and noncount nouns in the following paragraphs. Correct the mistakes and then rewrite the paragraphs. The first sentence has been done for you as an example.

(Informations) (are) easier to get with today's new technology. A news is transmitted around the world by TV satellites. Computers also make informations easier to get. Computers can help a person do his homeworks. Computer networks allow people to tell some news and give some advices. With computer mails a person can send a message with an electricity and a phone line.

There is a new kind of store in the United States now. Superstores are a combination of supermarkets and discount stores. Superstores have everything from foods to furnitures. At a superstore you can buy beverages like a coffee, a tea, or a milk. In the same store you can buy jewelrys, clothings, musics, and luggages. You can also buy things like a bread, a rice, a sugar, or a fruit. You should bring lots of moneys with you when you go to a superstore because there is a lot to buy. But one thing you can't buy at a superstore is the love.

This is an information gap activity. Work with a partner; one of you will look at Picture A while the other looks at Picture B. You will learn some of the prices of the items for sale in the Bag and Save grocery store while your partner learns other prices. Take turns asking each other the prices of the missing items.

PICTURE A

▶ **EXAMPLE:** *How much are eggs?* [$.89 per dozen.]

Use the pictures from Exercise 8 to take turns with your partner asking each other the price of more than one pound or item.

PICTURE B

▶ **EXAMPLE:** *How much are two cans of peaches?* [$1.98.]

Write sentences about your country using the *be* **+ adjective + noun pattern. Share the information about your country with your classmates.**

► **EXAMPLE:** popular sport

<u>Soccer is a popular sport in Brazil.</u>

1. popular sport

   _____

2. famous person

   _____

3. historic building

   _____

4. crowded city

   _____

5. delicious food

   _____

6. beautiful place to visit

   _____

7. popular actress

   _____

8. exciting holiday

   _____

9. expensive car

   _____

10. traditional musical instrument

   _____

THE VERB HAVE

Affirmative and Negative Statements, Questions and Short Answers, *Some/Any*

▶ **EXERCISE 1**   *(Focus 1, page 66)*

This is the Johnson family from Wisconsin. Jan Johnson, his wife, Jill, and their son Jack have many things for the cold and snowy Wisconsin winters.

This is the Sunshine family from California. Ray Sunshine and his wife, Tawny, and their daughter Malibu have many things for the warm California weather.

Using the cues, write sentences about what each family has.

▶ **EXAMPLE:** sled _Jack Johnson has a sled._

house _Both families have a house._

1. pet _____

_____

2. warm coat _____

_____

3. snow shovel _____

_____

4. hammock _____

_____

5. swimming pool _____

_____

6. porch _____

_____

7. child _____

_____

8. daughter _____

_____

9. son _____

_____

10. palm trees _____

_____

11. fireplace _____

_____

12. woodpile _____

_____

13. scarf _____

_____

14. wife _____

_____

15. sunglasses _____

_____

▶ **EXERCISE 2**   *(Focus 2, page 67)*

Use the pictures from Exercise 1 to complete the following sentences with true statements using the negative form of *have*. Follow the example.

▶ **EXAMPLE:** Jan Johnson _Jan Johnson doesn't have a daughter._____

1. Ray Sunshine _____

_____

2. The Johnson family _____

_____

3. Jan and Jill Johnson _____

_____

4. The Sunshines' house _____

_____

5. Jack Johnson _____

_____

6. The dog _____

_____

7. Malibu Sunshine _____

_____

8. The swimming pool _____

_____

9. The cat _____

_____

10. Tawny Sunshine _____

_____

▶ **EXERCISE 3**   *(Focus 3, page 68)*

With three classmates, take turns asking who has the following items in their homes. Record the short answers on the chart below.

	NAME	NAME	NAME
	_____	_____	_____
DO YOU HAVE . . .			
1. children?	_____	_____	_____
2. a TV?	_____	_____	_____
3. a car?	_____	_____	_____
4. a tent?	_____	_____	_____
5. a jet plane?	_____	_____	_____
6. a snow shovel?	_____	_____	_____
7. a watch?	_____	_____	_____
8. a sister?	_____	_____	_____
9. chopsticks?	_____	_____	_____
10. a swimming pool?	_____	_____	_____

Using the information from the pictures on pages 30 and 31, write the questions that go with the following answers.

► EXAMPLE: <u>Does Ray Sunshine have a son?</u>

No, he doesn't have a son.

1. _____

Yes, they have a swimming pool.

2. _____

Yes, he has a sled.

3. _____

No, they don't have a fireplace.

4. _____

Yes, she has a cat.

5. _____

Yes, they have a fireplace.

6. _____

No, they don't have a woodpile.

7. _____

Yes, California has palm trees.

8. _____

No, Wisconsin doesn't have palm trees.

9. _____

Yes, they have a hammock.

10. _____

Yes, Jack has a warm coat.

11. _____

Yes, she has sunglasses.

Fill in each blank in the conversation with *some* or *any*. The first one has been done for you as an example.

Kay: What are you doing this weekend?

Ray: I don't know. I have **(1)** _____ *some* _____ free time and I want to go to the movies, but I

don't have **(2)** _____ money.

Kay: Doesn't your father have **(3)** _____ money that he could lend you?

Ray: He has money, but he doesn't lend **(4)** _____ of it to me. He says that if I want

(5) _____ money, I have to work for it. I don't want to do **(6)** _____

work. I just want to have **(7)** _____ fun.

Kay: Doing **(8)** _____ work is not that hard. If you mow a couple of lawns, you can

make **(9)** _____ money fast.

Ray: I guess that isn't so difficult. Besides, I won't have **(10)** _____ fun if I stay home
all weekend.

Write a complete sentence, using the polite requests, for each cue.

► **Example:** books

       <u>Excuse me, do you have any books?</u>_____

  1. pencils _____

_____

  2. telephone _____

_____

  3. fountain pens _____

_____

  4. basketballs _____

_____

  5. restrooms _____

_____

6. photocopier _____

_____

7. Ashland University t-shirts _____

_____

8. notebooks _____

_____

9. computer disks _____

_____

10. comic books _____

_____

▶ **EXERCISE 7**   *(Focus 5, page 73)*

Look at the picture of the Ashland University bookstore. Using the requests in Exercise 6, take turns with your partner role-playing a customer and a salesclerk in the bookstore. The salesclerk should answer the polite requests according to what he or she can see in the picture.

Use the pictures of the Johnson and Sunshine families from Exercise 1 on pages 30 and 31 to write three sentences describing each person in the pictures. Use the verb *be* in one sentence in each group and the verb *have* in two sentences.

► **EXAMPLE:** The Johnsons

The Johnsons are short.

The Johnsons have black hair.

They have bangs.

JAN JOHNSON

1. _____

_____

2. _____

_____

3. _____

_____

JILL JOHNSON

1. _____

_____

2. _____

_____

3. _____

_____

JACK JOHNSON

1. _____

_____

2. _____

_____

3. _____

_____

THE SUNSHINES

1. _____

_____

2. _____

_____

3. _____

_____

RAY SUNSHINE

1. _____

   _____

2. _____

   _____

3. _____

   _____

TAWNY SUNSHINE

1. _____

   _____

2. _____

   _____

3. _____

   _____

MALIBU SUNSHINE

1. _____

   _____

2. _____

   _____

3. _____

   _____

UNIT 6

THIS/ THAT/ THESE/ THOSE

Possessives

Look at the pages from these two catalogues. Complete the sentences below using the correct demonstrative pronouns and the correct form of the verb *be*.

▶ EXAMPLE: _____Those_____ _____are_____ shoes.

1. _____ _____ a straw hat.

2. _____ _____ a thick sweater.

3. _____ _____ a cowboy hat.

4. _____ _____ shorts.

5. _____ _____ a polka-dot skirt.

6. _____ _____ shoes.

7. _____ _____ an expensive sweater.

8. _____ _____ long pants.

9. _____ _____ a necklace.

10. _____ _____
    a bracelet.

11. _____ _____
    a striped shirt.

Write questions using demonstratives for the nouns below. Then answer the questions. Use the words in the box below as clues.

► **Example:** near the speaker: newspapers, magazines

What are these?

These are things to read.

1. far from the speaker: couch, bed _____

_____

2. near the speaker: beef _____

_____

3. far from the speaker: doll _____

_____

4. near the speaker: IBM, Macintosh _____

_____

5. far from the speaker: green, yellow _____

_____

6. near the speaker: pine, maple _____

_____

7. near the speaker: apple _____

_____

8. far from the speaker: apartment, house _____

_____

9. near the speaker: can opener, toaster _____

_____

10. near the speaker: blanket _____

_____

things to read	doll	computers	kinds of furniture
kitchen appliances	trees	fruit	bedding
places to live	meat	colors	fruit

For each picture choose the correct caption and write it under the picture. The first one has been done for you as an example.

1. Mark's computer is new.
2. Erle's homework is incomplete.
3. Maya's car is a compact.
4. Mexico's flag has an eagle and a snake
5. Monique's car is luxurious.

6. Paulo's homework is finished.
7. James's computer is old.
8. The secretaries' desks are neat.
9. Canada's flag has a maple leaf on it.
10. The secretaries' desks are messy.

Maya's car is a compact.

_____

_____

_____

_____

_____

_____

_____

_____

_____

_____

_____

_____

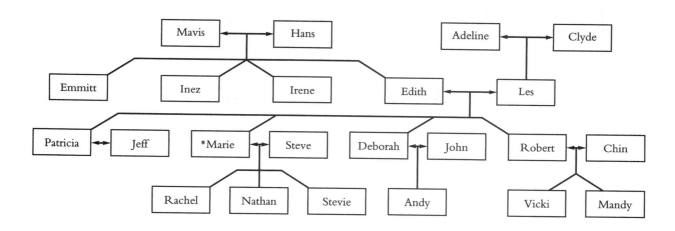

Write a sentence describing Marie's relationship with each person below.

▶ **EXAMPLE:** Nathan: Nathan is Marie's son.

1. Mandy _____

2. Mavis _____

3. Emmitt _____

4. Steve _____

5. Andy _____

6. Les _____

7. Rachel _____

8. Stevie _____

9. Hans _____

10. Chin _____

11. Jeff _____

12. Adeline and Clyde _____

13. Irene _____

14. Vicki _____

Fill in the blanks below to show your own family tree.

My Family Tree

_____   _____   _____   _____
Grandfather   Grandmother   Grandfather   Grandmother

              _____   _____
                  Mother   Father

                            _____
                                  Me

Answer the following questions about your family tree using complete sentences.

1. What is your mother's name? _____

_____

2. What is your father's name? _____

_____

3. What are your grandmothers' names? _____

_____

4. What are your grandfathers' names? _____

_____

Sun and Lee Park are brothers from Korea. They are studying English in the United States, but they are studying at different schools and in different programs. Sun is studying at a community college. Lee is studying in the intensive language program at a university. The brothers are talking on the phone and comparing the two different English programs.

Complete the dialogue using the correct possessive adjectives. The first one has been done for you as an example.

Sun: Hello, Lee. How are you? How is _____*your*_____ English program?

Lee: It's great. I have small classes. _____ classes have only 10 students.

Sun: That's good. _____ classes are very crowded. I have 30 students in my classes.

Lee: Does your program have a lab? We have a language lab. _____ lab has computers, tape recorders, and listening stations.

Sun: Yes, we have several labs. The computer lab is very large, and _____ computers are all new.

Lee: What about your teacher?

Sun: She is very nice. _____ name is Mrs. Nation. She always encourages us. She tells us _____ English is improving every day.

Lee: _____ teacher is a man. _____ name is Mr. Bahamonde. He also encourages us, but _____ tests are very difficult. He makes us work very hard. What about a textbook? Which book are you using?

Sun: We're using *Grammar Dimensions*. It's a very good book, and the activities are fun.

Lee: We're using *Grammar Dimensions,* too. I like it. How much does _____ program cost?

Sun: It's not too expensive.

Lee: _____ program is expensive. _____ cost is high, and I don't have any time to work.

Sun: You should try _____ program. It is only part-time.

▶ **EXERCISE 7**   *(Focus 4, page 91)*

Find one or two people in your class who fit the following descriptions. Write his/her/their name(s) on the lines at the right.

DESCRIPTION	NAMES
1. Her eyes are dark.	_____
	_____
2. His legs are long.	_____
	_____
3. Their ears are small.	_____
	_____

4. His hair is long. _____

_____

5. Her fingers are long. _____

_____

Complete the last five descriptions with your own words. Share your answers with your classmates.

6. Their hands are _____ _____

_____ _____

7. Our arms are _____ _____

_____ _____

8. My nose is _____ _____

_____ _____

9. Our _____ _____

_____ _____

10. My _____ _____

_____ _____

▶ **EXERCISE 8**   *(Focus 4, page 91)*

Match the people with their things. Then write a statement using the correct possessive pronoun.

1. Lucy is an accountant.	**A.** a book bag
2. Billy is a truck driver.	**B.** a calculator
3. Rudolfo and Juan are firemen.	**C.** a cash register
4. Scott is a plumber.	**D.** a fire hose
5. Toni is a singer.	**E.** a dog leash
6. Joyce is a dog trainer.	**F.** police badges
7. Julia and Thomas are police officers.	**G.** plans for a house
8. Angie is a student.	**H.** music
9. Roy is a salesclerk.	**I.** a truck
10. Isaac is an architect.	**J.** a football
11. Bruce is a football player.	**K.** a wrench

1. Lucy is an accountant. The calculator is hers. _____

2. _____

3. _____

4. _____

5. _____

6. _____

7. _____

8. _____

9. _____

10. _____

11. _____

▶ **EXERCISE 9**   *(Focus 5, page 94)*

The objects listed below belong to the people in the pictures. Using *Whose . . .?*, write questions to determine the objects' owners. Then write two answers, one with the possessive noun and one with the possessive pronoun.

James   **Ashley**   **Ginette and Jasmine**

▶ **EXAMPLE:** false teeth

Whose false teeth are these?   They're James' false teeth. _____

They're his. _____

1. mother _____

_____

2. notebooks _____

_____

3. boyfriends _____

_____

4. rocking chair _____

_____

5. tie _____

_____

6. bottle _____

_____

7. cane _____

_____

8. tape players _____

_____

9. toy _____

_____

10. cassette tapes _____

_____

11. glasses _____

_____

12. diaper _____

_____

EXERCISES FOR THE TOEFL® TEST

Units 4–6

Choose the *one* word or phrase that best completes each sentence.

1. The teacher _____ problem.
    (A) has a   (C) be a
    (B) has any   (D) have any

2. She works at an older school. They don't have computers at _____ school.
    (A) this   (C) these
    (B) that   (D) those

3. What's _____ ? It's _____ airplane.
    (A) these . . . an   (C) that . . . an
    (B) these . . . a   (D) that . . . some

4. She doesn't _____ new book.
    (A) has a   (C) has an
    (B) have an   (D) have a

5. Costa Rica and Brazil are _____ .
    (A) countrys   (C) country
    (B) a country   (D) countries

6. I _____ children.
    (A) no have any   (C) don't have any
    (B) don't have some   (D) doesn't has any

7. He has _____ homework in _____ class.
    (A) a . . . that   (C) any . . . that
    (B) one . . . these   (D) some . . . that

8. Do the children _____ toys? Yes, they do. The _____ are new.
    (A) has any . . . children's toys   (C) has a . . . children's toy
    (B) have any . . . children's toys (D) have any . . . children's toys

9. Ulrika _____ children.

    (A) has one   (C) have some

    (B) has two   (D) have any

10. They _____ bread.

    (A) have a   (C) have any

    (B) has some   (D) have some

11. _____ short brown hair.

    (A) That girl no has   (C) The girl doesn't has

    (B) Those girls doesn't have   (D) That girl doesn't have

12. There are two _____ .

    (A) deer   (C) mans

    (B) deers   (D) man

13. I have _____ sugar. There isn't _____ more.

    (A) some . . . any   (C) no . . . any

    (B) some . . . some   (D) a . . . some

14. Do the dogs have food? No, the _____ are empty.

    (A) dog's bowls   (C) dog's

    (B) dogs' bowls   (D) dogs' bowl

15. The cat has a bed. _____ bed is comfortable.

    (A) It's   (C) Your

    (B) Its   (D) Their

Find the *one* underlined word or phrase that must be changed for the sentence to be grammatically correct.

16. Mickey <u>is</u> <u>a</u> famous <u>mice</u> at the <u>Florida</u> attraction Disney World.
              A B   C   D

17. <u>That</u> is strange. <u>That man</u> <u>has</u> <u>three watchs</u> on his wrist.
   A   B   C   D

18. <u>That house</u> <u>have</u> heat in all of <u>the</u> rooms except <u>the</u> garage.
     A   B   C   D

19. <u>How many</u> does <u>a hamburger</u> cost at <u>that</u> new restaurant in <u>Orlando</u>?
     A   B   C   D

20. <u>I have</u> a daughter. <u>My</u> <u>daughter's hair</u> is black like <u>my</u>.
    A   B   C   D

21. <u>That</u> food is too spicy. <u>Her</u> has to drink <u>some water</u> with <u>her dinner</u>.
    A   B   C   D

22. <u>Who</u> paper is <u>this</u>? It has <u>Joan's name</u> on it. I think it is <u>hers</u>.
    A   B   C   D

23. Ludmilla <u>doesn't have</u> a book. Please give that book to <u>she</u>. <u>It is</u> <u>hers</u>.
                 A   **B** **C** **D**

24. <u>Whose</u> <u>homeworks are</u> on the table? I think <u>it's Sancho's</u> homework. He <u>doesn't have his</u>.
       A   **B**   **C**   **D**

25. <u>Do you have</u> <u>any biographies</u>? Yes, we have many books about <u>the lifes</u> of famous <u>people</u>.
       A   **B**   **C**   **D**

THERE IS / THERE ARE

A/An Versus *The*

▶ **EXERCISE 1**   *(Focus 1, page 100)*

Look at the picture of Farmer Dell's farm. Underline the sentence in each pair that best describes this picture.

▶ **EXAMPLE:** A farm is in this picture.	<u>There is a farm in this picture.</u>
1. There is a pig in the mud.	A pig is in the mud.
2. A horse is in the barn.	There is a horse in the barn.
3. Chickens are in the chicken coop.	There are chickens in the coop.
4. There is hay in the barn.	Hay is in the barn.
5. The goat is beside the barn.	There's a goat beside the barn.
6. The farmer is in his truck.	There's a farmer in the truck.
7. There are ducks on the pond.	Ducks are on the pond.
8. There's a rooster on the chicken coop.	A rooster is on the chicken coop.
9. There is some corn in the field.	Some corn is in the field.
10. Two cows are in the barn.	There are two cows in the barn.

Farmer McDonald has some problems on his farm. There are twelve things wrong with this picture. Write affirmative statements about the picture with *There + be* using the cues given.

► **EXAMPLE:** horse   There is a horse on the roof.

1. pig _____

2. chickens _____

3. corn _____

4. goat, duck, rooster _____

5. TV _____

6. electricity _____

7. cows _____

8. hat _____

9. glasses _____

10. dog _____

11. furniture _____

Cecilia is choosing a college. She likes the academic program and teachers at New College, but she wants to have more services and facilities. Cecilia made a list of things she would like New College to have. Change the list into negative statements using *There + be.*

► **EXAMPLE:** campus-wide e-mail <u>There's no campus-wide e-mail.</u>

1. gym _____

_____

2. job counselors _____

_____

3. college radio station _____

_____

4. public transportation into town _____

_____

5. cultural events _____

_____

6. language lab _____

_____

7. math tutor _____

_____

8. drugstore close to campus _____

_____

9. quiet places to study _____

_____

10. soccer team _____

_____

Imagine that you are trying to choose a school or college. Using the cues, write questions about the services and facilities available at the school.

► **EXAMPLE:** job counselors <u>Are there any job counselors?</u>

1. academic counselors _____

_____

2. library _____

_____

3. scholarships _____

_____

4. financial aid money _____

_____

5. sports teams _____

_____

6. bookstore _____

_____

7. student clubs _____

_____

8. tutors _____

_____

9. dorms _____

_____

10. entertainment _____

_____

Choose the definite or the indefinite article *(a, an,* or *the)* for each blank. The first one has been done for you as an example.

A Friend's Birthday

Cristina went to _____ a _____ bakery to buy a cake. _____ bakery is new—it opened just last month. _____ cake is for _____ friend's birthday.

_____ friend's name is Lola. She is from Colombia. This is _____ first birthday Lola is celebrating without her family. Cristina doesn't want Lola to feel bad because she isn't with her family.

Cristina wants to buy Lola _____ special present. But _____ present can't cost too much because Cristina doesn't have much money. Cristina is looking for _____ umbrella. She thinks that _____ umbrella will make _____ practical and beautiful gift.

When she finds _____ perfect umbrella, she tries to wrap it in colorful paper, but _____ umbrella is _____ difficult present to wrap. Finally, Cristina just puts _____ big bow on _____ umbrella.

When Cristina gives Lola _____ present and _____ cake, Lola is surprised. She is happy to have _____ good friend like Cristina.

SIMPLE PRESENT TENSE

Affirmative and Negative Statements, Time Expressions:

Like/Want/Need

▶ **EXERCISE 1**   *(Focus 1, page 118)*

Read the stories about Thad and Cara and then underline each of the present tense verbs. The first one has been done for you as an example.

Thad Thrifty always <u>tries</u> to save money and resources. Before he goes grocery shopping, he checks the advertisements in the newspaper and cuts out coupons to save money. He uses cold water to wash his clothes to save energy and dries them outside on a clothesline when the weather is nice. He conserves electricity whenever possible. For example, he always turns off lights when he leaves a room.

Cara Careless spends money all the time. She buys food because it looks tasty. She forgets to plan meals, so she eats out a lot. She wastes water when she washes her car. She always forgets to turn off her stereo when she leaves the house. She always dries her clothes in the dryer, even in warm weather.

Choose the correct word given in parentheses to complete the story. Be sure the subject and the verb agree. The first one has been done for you as an example.

I _____ *want* _____ (want, wants) you to meet my friend Herb Ban and his wife, Sunny. They _____ (live, lives) in the city. Herb _____ (like, likes) the city because his apartment is close to his job. Herb _____ (walk, walks) to work every morning. He _____ (work, works) in the building across the street from his apartment. In the winter, Herb _____ (go, goes) to work without getting cold. He just _____ (walk, walks) through a tunnel that _____ (go, goes) between the two buildings.

Sunny, Herb's wife, _____ (think, thinks) the city is all right, but she _____ (prefer, prefers) the country. Sunny _____ (enjoy, enjoys) camping in the mountains. Every summer, they _____ (camp, camps) in Montana for two weeks. Herb always _____ (complain, complains) about the mosquitoes. He _____ (hate, hates) mosquitoes.

Personally, I _____ (want, wants) to live in the country, but I'm like Herb. I _____ (work, works) in the city.

Do you try to save money and energy? Check the statements below that are generally true for you. Then choose a partner and compare your answers with your partner's. Write true statements about your and your partner's habits.

► **EXAMPLE:** *I save coupons.*
Sam reads the labels carefully before he buys something.
We both check advertisements for sales on food or clothing.

1. ___ I check advertisements for sales on food or clothing.

2. ___ I save coupons.

3. ___ I read labels carefully before I buy something.

4. ___ I plan my meals.

5. ___ I conserve water.

6. ___ I wash my clothes in cold water.

7. ___ I dry my clothes on a clothesline.

8. ___ I eat at restaurants most of the time.

9. ___ I waste water when I brush my teeth.

10. ___ I forget to turn off lights when I leave the room.

11. ___ I always dry my clothes in a dryer.

Write statements about a family member using ten of the verbs below. Read the statements to your partner. Try to say each verb correctly in the third person. If possible, record yourself on tape and listen to your pronunciation.

make	clean	wash	work	iron	rush	walk
fight	run	fix	sleep	swim	mix	read
watch	help	freeze	eat	like	wish	cook

► **EXAMPLE:** <u>My brother fights with my little sister.</u>

1. _____

2. _____

3. _____

4. _____

5. _____

6. _____

7. _____

8. _____

9. _____

10. _____

Finish the story with the correct form of each verb given in parentheses. Watch your spelling. Then read the story out loud. If possible, record yourself and listen for the correct pronunciation of the verbs. The first one has been done for you as an example.

Norman _____*goes*_____ (go) to work on the bus. He _____ (hurry) to the bus stop because he doesn't want to miss the bus. Norman _____ (enjoy) his work, but he _____ (worry) when he is late. His boss _____ (have) strict rules about being on time.

Norman _____ (work) for a toy company. He _____ (test) toys. Every morning Norman _____ (have) a box of new toys on his desk. First he _____ (empty) the box and _____ (look) at the toys he will test. Then Norman _____ (play) with the toys. He _____ (try) them out.

After he _____ (see) what a toy _____ (do), Norman _____ (write) a report about the toy. The report _____ (say) what age child the toy is best for. It also _____ (tell) about any possible dangers to children. Then Norman _____ (send) his report and the toy to his boss.

Using the cues, make two true statements about yourself by adding a time expression or a frequency expression. Skip the statements that are not true for you.

► EXAMPLE: go to school <u>I go to school three days a week.</u>

<u>I go to school in the morning.</u>

1. go to school _____

_____

2. eat pizza _____

_____

3. see your family _____

_____

4. drink water _____

_____

5. call your mother _____

_____

6. cook a meal _____

_____

7. watch TV _____

_____

8. go to the dentist _____

_____

9. eat Chinese food _____

_____

10. wash your clothes _____

_____

11. pay your bills _____

_____

12. read the newspaper _____

_____

Make a list of things that you usually do in each of the following time periods. Then write sentences about your activities using *in, at, on,* or *no preposition*.

► EXAMPLE: summer

take a vacation   In the summer I usually take a vacation.

go camping   I usually *go camping* in the summer.

SUMMER

1. _____

2. _____

3. _____

MONDAY

1. _____

2. _____

3. _____

NOON

1. _____

2. _____

3. _____

WEEKENDS

1. _____

2. _____

3. _____

DECEMBER

1. _____

2. _____

3. _____

Ask your partner the following questions using the information in Exercise 7 to help with the answers.

► **EXAMPLE:** **A:** *What do you usually do in the summer?*
          B: *I usually take a vacation. I usually go camping in the summer.*

1. What do you usually do in the summer?
2. What do you usually do on Mondays?
3. What do you usually do at noon?
4. What do you usually do on weekends?
5. What do you usually do in December?

Don and Ron are brothers. They are different in some ways and the same in others. Look at the information about Don and Ron and, using the cues given, make negative sentences on the next page.

RON

Ron is a park ranger; he works outdoors. He drives a pickup truck and lives in a house. Ron likes to stay healthy. He likes exercise, but he doesn't like jogging. He prefers playing volleyball with his friends. Ron doesn't like basketball or movies. He doesn't smoke, and he is a vegetarian.

DON

Don is an accountant; he works in a big office downtown. He has a sports car and lives in an apartment. Still, Don likes to stay healthy. He likes exercise, but he doesn't like jogging. He enjoys playing basketball with his friends. He likes to do active things. He doesn't like going to the movies. He is a vegetarian, and he doesn't smoke.

► **EXAMPLE:** _Don doesn't work outside._

Don and Ron don't eat meat.

1. work inside _____

_____

2. live in a house _____

_____

3. smoke _____

_____

4. have a sports car _____

_____

5. play volleyball _____

_____

6. likes jogging _____

_____

7. drive a pickup truck _____

_____

8. live in an apartment _____

_____

9. like movies _____

_____

10. like basketball _____

_____

Read the list of activities below and ask yourself whether good parents do each of them. Choose yes or no and then complete each statement, making it affirmative or negative.

	YES	NO

▶ **EXAMPLE:** let their children stay up late every night ____ __×__

       Good parents don't let their children stay up late every night.

1. play in the street ____ ____

_____

2. make their children do chores ____ ____

_____

3. give their children an allowance (weekly money) ____ ____

_____

4. let their children watch TV five hours every day ____ ____

_____

5. leave their children at home alone ____ ____

_____

6. give their children cigarettes ____ ____

_____

7. feed their children healthy food ____ ____

_____

8. help their children with their homework ____ ____

_____

9. let their children go to the library ____ ____

_____

10. know their children's friends ____ ____

_____

You and your partner are going to take a trip to Europe together. Make a list of all the things you plan to take with you and the places you plan to see. Then, for each item on your list, decide whether you want, like, or need to take it or see it. Then share your vacation plans with another group.

▶ **EXAMPLE:**

THINGS	TO DO
Write: sweaters—need camera—want	see Paris—need take photos—want
Then tell another pair: We need sweaters. We want a camera.	We need to see Paris. We want to take photos.

THINGS	TO DO
1.	1.
2.	2.
3.	3.
4.	4.
5.	5.
6.	6.
7.	7.
8.	8.

UNIT 9

SIMPLE PRESENT TENSE

Yes/No Questions, Adverbs of Frequency, Wh-Questions

▶ **EXERCISE 1**   (Focus 1, page 140)

Using the cues, write yes/no questions. Then ask your partner the questions. Write down his or her short answers.

▶ **EXAMPLE:** watch sports on TV _____Do you watch sports on TV?_____

_____Yes, I do._____ or _____No, I don't._____

1. watch movies on TV _____

_____

2. sing in the shower _____

_____

3. work _____

_____

4. have a hobby _____

_____

5. believe in ghosts _____

_____

6. cook your own meals _____

_____

7. like to dance _____

_____

8. take vacations _____

_____

9. have a pet _____

_____

10. play chess _____

_____

► **EXERCISE 2**   *(Focus 1, page 140)*

Change partners. Ask your new partner about his or her first partner, using the cues from Exercise 1. Record his or her short answers.

► **EXAMPLE:** watch sports on TV *Does Mohamad watch sports on TV?* ____

Yes, he does. _____

1. watch movies on TV _____

_____

2. sing in the shower _____

_____

3. work _____

_____

4. have a hobby _____

_____

5. believe in ghosts _____

_____

6. cook his/her own meals _____

_____

7. like to dance _____

_____

8. take vacations _____

_____

9. have a pet _____

_____

10. play chess _____

_____

The list below shows healthy and unhealthy habits and adverbs of frequency. Check the box for each that is true for you.

Habits	Always	Almost Always	Usually	Often; Frequently	Sometimes	Seldom; Rarely	Never
1. exercise							
2. eat fresh vegetables							
3. sleep eight hours							
4. relax							
5. drink water							
6. take vitamins							
7. eat junk food							
8. drink alcohol							
9. drive too fast							
10. smoke cigarettes							
11. get sunburned							

Adverbs of Frequency

Using your answers from Exercise 3, write sentences about your healthy and unhealthy habits. Compare your answers with those of your classmates.

▶ EXAMPLE: <u>I frequently exercise.</u>

1. _____

2. _____

3. _____

4. _____

5. _____

6. _____

7. _____

8. _____

9. _____

10. _____

11. _____

▶ **EXERCISE 5** *(Focus 4, page 148)*

Fanny Fad, a reporter for *Teen Star* magazine, interviewed these teenage stars. Read each article and then finish the questions Fanny asked, using the cues. The first one has been done for you as an example.

Chris Crash, 15

Chris Crash likes to skateboard. He likes skateboarding because it is a fast sport. Chris lives in California. He practices skateboarding every day after school. He learns new skateboard tricks by studying other skateboarders. Chris wants to act in a skateboard movie.

1. What <u>do you like to do?</u> _____

2. Why _____

3. Where _____

4. How often _____

5. When _____

6. How _____

7. What _____

Suzy Flex, 13

Suzy likes gymnastics. She practices hard because she wants to compete in the summer Olympics. She rehearses her gymnastic routines twice a day at the gym. She practices at 5:00 every morning and 4:30 every afternoon. She learns new routines with the help of her coach.

1. What _____

2. Why _____

3. How often _____

4. Where _____

5. What time _____

6. How _____

7. When _____

▶ **EXERCISE 6**   *(Focus 4, page 148)*

Write the question that goes with each of the answers. Use the underlined words as cues.

▶ **EXAMPLE:** <u>Where does your mother live?</u> _____

My mother lives <u>in Brazil</u>.

1. _____

I call my parents <u>once a week</u> on Saturday.

2. _____

My parents <u>wait</u> for my call.

3. _____

They wait <u>because they know I will always call on time</u>.

4. _____

I call at <u>8 P.M.</u>

5. _____

My brother lives <u>in Brazil</u> also.

6. _____

<u>He is a clerk</u> in a government office.

7. _____

He works <u>in Brasilia</u>.

8. _____

My parents live <u>in São Paulo</u>.

9. _____

My brother lives in Brasilia <u>because it is the capital of Brazil</u>.

10. _____

He <u>goes</u> to São Paulo on holidays.

▶ **EXERCISE 7**   *(Focus 5, page 150)*

Read the story. Write "who or whom" questions to go with each answer, using the underlined words as cues.

Jill, Mandy, and Joy are roommates. They share an apartment near the college they are attending. They share the responsibilities for the apartment, and they also do many things together.

Jill drives Mandy and Joy to school every day. Joy makes dinner on weekdays, and Mandy makes dinner on weekends. Joy's responsibility is to take out the trash on Mondays. Mandy puts out the recycling on Wednesdays. Jill washes her car on Saturdays.

Usually their friends Sam, Roy, and George eat dinner with them on Saturdays. Mandy and Jill also play tennis together.

▶ **EXAMPLE:**   <u>Who are Mandy's roommates?</u>

<u>Jill and Joy</u> are Mandy's roommates.

1. _____

<u>Mandy, Joy, and Jill</u> share an apartment.

2. _____

<u>Mandy, Jill, and Joy</u> go to school.

3. _____

<u>Jill</u> drives the car.

4. _____

<u>Jill</u> drives Mandy and Joy to school every day.

5. _____

<u>Joy</u> cooks dinner on Tuesday.

6. _____

<u>Mandy</u> prepares dinner on the weekends.

7. _____

<u>Joy</u> takes out the trash.

8. _____

<u>Mandy</u> puts out the recycling.

9. _____

<u>Jill</u> washes her own car.

10. _____

They meet <u>Sam, George, and Roy</u> on Saturday night.

11. _____

<u>Mandy and Jill</u> play tennis.

► **EXERCISE 8**   *(Focus 5, page 150)*

Read the following questions. Write "I" in front of the question if it is informal. Write "F" in front of the question if it is formal.

► EXAMPLE: _____F_____ Whom do the teachers help?

1. ___ Who will you give the flowers to?

2. ___ Whom can I expect to meet at the party?

3. ___ Who will receive this package?

4. ___ Who has my new hairdryer?

5. ___ Who wants ice cream?

6. ___ Who studies on weekends?

7. ___ Whom do you sit next to in class?

8. ___ Who speaks three languages?

Read each question. If it is correct write "C" in front of it. If it is incorrect write "I" in front of it and rewrite the question correctly.

► **EXAMPLE:** _____I_____ How you pronounce "toothache"?

   How do you pronounce "toothache"?

1. ___ How do you spell "sincerely"?

_____

2. ___ How you say the opposite of "tired"?

_____

3. ___ How to pronounce "potato"?

_____

4. ___ What means "illogical"?

_____

5. ___ What the word "frantic" means?

_____

6. ___ How do you say the opposite of freedom?

_____

7. ___ How spell "Wednesday"?

_____

8. ___ How you pronounce your name?

_____

9. ___ What do means "ethical"?

_____

10. ___ How you say a little wet?

_____

Using the appropriate questions, ask your partner about the items listed below. If neither of you knows the correct answer, look it up in a bilingual dictionary. Follow the example.

► **EXAMPLE: Q:** *What is the opposite of boring?*
   A: *Interesting.*

OPPOSITES	SPELLING	PRONUNCIATION
boring	your name	through
relaxed	the capital of the United States	Illinois
winter	the President's name	your name

MEANING	DESCRIPTION
neither	a thing that a baby drinks from
annoy	the square thing you put into a computer
obligatory	a chair with no back, just legs

EXERCISES FOR THE TOEFL® TEST

Units 7-9

Choose the *one* word or phrase that best completes each sentence.

1. _____ live in Baltimore?
   - (A) Do she
   - (B) Do you
   - (C) Does they
   - (D) Do he

2. Carmela gets home _____ 5:00 and prepares dinner.
   - (A) at
   - (B) in
   - (C) on
   - (D) to

3. Do you _____ work on Saturday? Yes, I _____ work on Saturdays.
   - (A) seldom . . . always
   - (B) ever . . . seldom
   - (C) never . . . always
   - (D) ever . . . always

4. _____ a good restaurant near my apartment.
   - (A) There are
   - (B) Is it
   - (C) There is
   - (D) This

5. _____ any mail for me today?
   - (A) Is
   - (B) Are there
   - (C) Are
   - (D) Is there

6. _____ the bookstore open on Saturday?
   - (A) When does
   - (B) What time do
   - (C) Who does
   - (D) What does

7. Forrest Bowlins is a banker. He _____ people's money.
   - (A) manages
   - (B) manage
   - (C) have to
   - (D) wants a

8. Sheldon _____ a nap after school.
   - (A) take
   - (B) does
   - (C) wanting
   - (D) takes

9. Once a week, _____ Fridays, Diane goes dancing.
    (A) in   (C) on
    (B) at   (D) the

10. I celebrate my birthday _____ May 19th.
    (A) on the   (C) the
    (B) in   (D) on

11. A healthy person _____ eat hamburgers every day.
    (A) don't   (C) no
    (B) doesn't   (D) any

12. Chieko _____ want to miss class.
    (A) no   (C) don't
    (B) not   (D) doesn't

13. Enriqueta and Jo _____ about their friend.
    (A) worried   (C) are worried
    (B) are worry   (D) worrying

14. Charlie is always tired. He _____ sleep very well at night.
    (A) no   (C) not
    (B) isn't   (D) doesn't

15. _____ do you get to school? _____ .
    (A) How . . . I take by bus   (C) How . . . I take the bus
    (B) What . . . By bus   (D) What . . . I ride

Identify the *one* underlined word or phrase that must be changed for the sentence to be grammatically correct.

16. She <u>makes plans</u> for her vacation <u>on December</u>. She decides <u>to go to the mountains</u>, even
         A   **B**   **C**
    though she likes <u>to go the beach</u>.
                  D

17. <u>There</u> <u>aren't</u> <u>any milk</u> <u>in the refrigerator</u>.
    A   **B**   **C**   **D**

18. The <u>Italian restaurant</u> <u>is open</u>, but <u>it no have</u> <u>any linguine</u> today.
          A   **B**   **C**   **D**

19. <u>The sun</u> <u>rises always</u> in the east and <u>sets</u> <u>in the west</u>.
    A   **B**   **C**   **D**

20. <u>Many</u> people <u>in India</u> <u>don't eats</u> meat; they <u>eat only</u> vegetables.
    A   **B**   **C**   **D**

21. <u>In the winter</u>, they <u>go for ski</u> <u>in the mountains</u> <u>in Colorado</u>.
    A   **B**   **C**   **D**

22. <u>Is there</u> anything for the children <u>to do</u> <u>in the summer</u>? They <u>go to swimming</u>.
      A   B   C   D

23. <u>I need</u> <u>to do a phone call</u> before <u>we make a decision</u> about <u>the new car</u>.
     A   B   C   D

24. Blanca <u>doesn't goes</u> <u>to the university</u> <u>on Fridays</u> <u>in December</u>.
             A   B   C   D

25. <u>There is</u> a word <u>I don't know</u>. <u>What means</u> sibling? <u>It means</u> a brother or a sister.
     A   B   C   D

UNIT 10

IMPERATIVES AND PREPOSITIONS OF DIRECTION

▶ **EXERCISE 1** *(Focus 1, page 158)*

Using the pictures and cues, write affirmative, negative, or polite imperative sentences.

▶ **EXAMPLE:** Affirmative: _Stay away!_ _____

          Negative: _Don't touch!_ _____

1.   Affirmative: _____

              _____

          Polite: _____

              _____

2.   Affirmative: _____

              _____

          Polite: _____

              _____

3.   Affirmative: _____

              _____

          Negative: _____

              _____

4. Affirmative: _____

   _____

   Polite: _____

   _____

5. Affirmative: _____

   _____

   Polite: _____

   _____

6. Affirmative: _____

   _____

   Negative: _____

   _____

7. Affirmative: _____

   _____

   Polite: _____

   _____

8. Affirmative: _____

   _____

   Negative: _____

   _____

Study each of the following examples and write the function of each imperative next to the example.

FUNCTIONS

- Giving advice
- Giving an order
- Warning of danger
- Making a polite request
- Politely offering something
- Giving directions

► **EXAMPLE:** Do not expose to heat. Keep out of the reach of children. Avoid freezing.

     Warning of danger

1. Mix the butter and the sugar well. Beat in the molasses. Add the flour, soda, cloves, cinnamon, ginger, and salt.

_____

2. Danger: Harmful if swallowed. Read caution on back label carefully.

_____

3. Bring me that report.

_____

4. Please have some more pot roast.

_____

5. Please gift wrap this.

_____

6. Remember to call if you have a problem. Eat well and get enough sleep.

_____

Check "yes" if the imperative is appropriate in the situation. Check "no" if it is not appropriate. Check "depends" if you think it could be appropriate in certain situations.

Situation	Imperative	Yes	No	Depends
► EXAMPLE: Son to father:	Example: Give me the car keys!		x	
1. Police officer to teenager:	Don't drive so fast!			
2. Student to teacher:	Tell me the answer.			
3. Patient to doctor:	Fill out these insurance forms.			
4. Lawyer to client:	Don't say anything to the police.			
5. Employee to boss:	Give me the report!			
6. Dentist to patient:	Brush your teeth three times a day.			
7. Roommate to roommate:	Answer the phone!			

► **EXERCISE 4** *(Focus 3, page 162)*

For each inappropriate imperative from Exercise 3, rewrite the imperative in the appropriate form.

► EXAMPLE: Dad, please give me the car keys.

_____

_____

_____

_____

_____

Read the following sentences. For each, if the sentence is correct, write "C" in front of it. If the sentence is incorrect, write "I" in front of it and rewrite the sentence to make it correct.

► **EXAMPLE:** __I__ Debbie lives on an apartment building.

   Debbie lives in an apartment building.

1. ___ She works in the business district. _____

_____

2. ___ Debbie's office is out of the seventh floor. _____

_____

3. ___ Every morning Debbie is late for work, so she runs on her house. _____

_____

4. ___ She drives out of her driveway. _____

_____

5. ___ She turns left out of her neighborhood and gets on the freeway. _____

_____

6. ___ Debbie gets at the freeway when she gets downtown. _____

_____

7. ___ She rushes out of her car and goes to the elevator. _____

_____

8. ___ She runs at the elevator. _____

_____

9. ___ She gets off on the seventh floor just in time. _____

_____

10. ___ When her boss arrives, Debbie is off her desk. _____

_____

You need three people to do this activity. The first person whispers the directions listed below to the second person. The second person must follow the directions. The third person writes down what she or he sees the second person do. You should begin outside of your classroom.

► **EXAMPLE:** Whisper: *Walk into the class.*

Write: <u>Joseph walks into the class.</u>

1. Walk into the classroom. ⸺⸺⸺⸺⸺⸺⸺⸺⸺⸺

2. Run to the desk. ⸺⸺⸺⸺⸺⸺⸺⸺⸺⸺⸺⸺

3. Put your book on the desk. ⸺⸺⸺⸺⸺⸺⸺⸺⸺⸺

4. Tiptoe away from the desk. ⸺⸺⸺⸺⸺⸺⸺⸺⸺⸺

5. Walk back to the desk. ⸺⸺⸺⸺⸺⸺⸺⸺⸺⸺⸺

6. Take your book off of the desk. ⸺⸺⸺⸺⸺⸺⸺⸺⸺

7. Jump out of the classroom. ⸺⸺⸺⸺⸺⸺⸺⸺⸺⸺

Change roles. The first person can change the order of the activities.

Match the sentence with the activity in the picture.

1. The boy walks through the mud.
2. The girl slides down the slide.
3. The joggers run along the path.
4. The girl walks around the mud.
5. The children walk across the balance beam.
6. The children climb up the ladder.
7. The woman runs past the man.
8. The old man walks over the bridge.
9. The boy crawls through the tunnel.
10. The girl swings across the bars.
11. The boy climbs up the bars.

QUANTIFIERS

Look at the picture of the five food groups. Decide which foods are count and which are noncount nouns. Write the name of each food in the proper category.

COUNT	NONCOUNT
crackers	milk

Look at what Wendy Weightlifter and Skinny Sarah had for breakfast and lunch and then complete the sentences below using *many, a lot of, some, a few, a little, few, no, much, very little,* **or** *any.* **There is more than one correct answer for some of the blanks. Compare your answers with a classmate. The first one has been done for you.**

WENDY WEIGHTLIFTER		SKINNY SARAH	
BREAKFAST	**LUNCH**	**BREAKFAST**	**LUNCH**
four eggs	chicken	yogurt	vegetable soup
orange juice	onion rings	cup of coffee	milk
bacon	four apples	bagel	salad
three pieces of toast	three sodas		grapes

Wendy had **(1)** _____*some*_____ eggs for breakfast. She also drank **(2)** _____

orange juice. She ate **(3)** _____ bacon. Finally, she ate **(4)** _____ toast.

Sarah didn't eat **(5)** _____ for breakfast. She had **(6)** _____ yogurt. She

drank **(7)** _____ coffee and ate a bagel with **(8)** _____ jam.

Wendy also had a big lunch. She ate **(9)** _____ chicken, **(10)** _____

onion rings, and **(11)** _____ apples. She also drank **(12)** _____ soda.

Sarah didn't have **(13)** _____ chicken for lunch. She had **(14)** _____

soup,   **(15)** _____ salad,   and   **(16)** _____ grapes.   She   drank

(17) _____ milk.

Write three sentences about what you ate yesterday, using the quantifiers in the directions from Exercise 2.

_____

_____

_____

Wendy is training for a bodybuilding competition. She needs to lose some weight before the competition, and she has decided the best way to lose it would be to go to training camp. However, Wendy is not very happy at camp. Finish the letter she wrote to her mother with *a few, a little, few,* **or** *little.* **The first one has been done for you.**

Dear Mom,

I hope everything is ok at home. I'm having _____*a few*_____ problems here at training camp. I'm glad that I have only **(1)** _____ more time here. I'm ready to go home.

First, I wish we could have **(2)** _____ more food. There is so **(3)** _____ food at breakfast that I'm starving by 10:00. All I had for breakfast was **(4)** _____ grapes, **(5)** _____ milk, and a piece of toast with **(6)** _____ margarine.

Another problem is the exercise program. We are always doing something: lifting weights, walking, swimming, or riding bikes. We have **(7)** _____ time to relax. At the end of the day I have **(8)** _____ energy. I can barely make it into bed. Then we have so **(9)** _____ hours to sleep. They wake us up at 6:00, and we go to bed at 10:00. I am exhausted.

The only good thing is that I've made **(10)** _____ friends. There are three girls in my cabin who are also trying to lose **(11)** _____ weight for the competition.

I will be home in three days. Thank goodness I have only **(12)** _____ more time here. Maybe I can lose **(13)** _____ weight in **(14)** _____ more days here.

Your daughter,

Wendy

**Write the questions about what Wendy and Sarah ate, using *How much* or *How many*.
Refer to Exercise 2 if you need to.**

▶ EXAMPLE: How many onion rings did she eat?

   She ate twelve onion rings.

1. _____

She drank one cup of coffee for breakfast.

2. _____

She didn't have any hot dogs for lunch.

3. _____

She drank a lot of orange juice for breakfast.

4. _____

She didn't eat much for breakfast. She ate just a little.

5. _____

She had a little vegetable soup.

6. _____

She ate four apples for lunch.

7. _____

She didn't eat any grapes for lunch.

8. _____

She didn't have any soup for lunch.

9. _____

She ate a little yogurt for breakfast.

10. _____

She had a little milk at lunch.

Wendy is home from training camp and wants to go grocery shopping. Her mother told her to make a shopping list. Look at the things Wendy is thinking of buying and write Wendy's list using the correct measure word. The first one has been done for you as an example.

1. <u>a loaf of bread</u>

2. _____

3. _____

4. _____

5. _____

6. _____

7. _____

8. _____

9. _____

10. _____

11. _____

12. _____

U N I T 1 2

ADVERBS OF MANNER

Take turns with your partner asking the following questions. Answer using complete sentences. Write each other's answers.

▶ **EXAMPLE:** **A:** Are you calm or nervous when you take a test?

B: _____ I'm calm when I take a test. _____

1. Are you happy or sad when you get your grades? _____

_____

2. Are you grumpy or cheerful when you wake up in the morning? _____

_____

3. Are you clothes loose or tight? _____

_____

4. Are you a heavy or a light exerciser? _____

_____

5. Are you shy or outgoing when you meet a new person? _____

_____

6. Are you slow or quick when you walk somewhere? _____

_____

7. Are you careful or careless when you drive? _____

_____

Write answers to the following questions about your partner, using complete sentences.

▶ **EXAMPLE:** Does your partner take tests calmly?

   <u>Yes, she (or he) takes tests calmly.</u>

1. Does your partner get his (or her) grades happily? _____

_____

2. Does your partner wake up grumpily? _____

_____

3. Do your partner's clothes fit loosely? _____

_____

4. Does your partner exercise heavily? _____

_____

5. Does your partner meet new people easily? _____

_____

6. Does your partner walk quickly? _____

_____

7. Does your partner drive carelessly? _____

_____

Using the information from this story, fill in the blanks in the second story using adverbs instead of adjectives. The first one has been done for you.

Mom was early coming home because her shopping trip was terrible. She was enthusiastic when she left the house because there were many new clothes she wanted to buy.

First she tried on a blue skirt. The skirt looked good, but the fit was terrible. It was loose. So she tried on a black skirt, but it was tight. When she took the skirt off she was careless, and the zipper broke. She tried to be careful when she fixed the zipper, but it got stuck. She couldn't get the skirt on or off. She became anxious and pulled on the zipper, but it still wouldn't move. She didn't know what to do. Even though she felt shy, she called for a saleswoman. The saleswoman was glad to help. She tried to unzip the skirt, but she was also unsuccessful. Mom was brave. She was calm as she waited. The saleswoman got some scissors and made a neat cut near the zipper. Mom was quick to leave the store.

Mom came home _____*early*_____ because her shopping trip went _____. She left _____ because there were many new clothes she wanted to buy.

First she tried on a blue skirt. The skirt looked good, but it fit _____. It fit _____. So she tried on a black skirt, but it fit _____. She took the skirt off _____, and the zipper broke. She tried to fix the zipper _____, but it got stuck. She couldn't get the skirt on or off. She pulled _____ on the zipper, but it still wouldn't move. She didn't know what to do. She _____ called for a saleswoman. The saleswoman _____ helped. She tried _____ to unzip the skirt. Mom stood _____ and waited _____. The saleswoman got some scissors and cut _____ near the zipper. Mom left the store _____.

What do you know about the different jobs below? Using the cues, write two sentences for each job. One sentence focuses on the person; the other sentence focuses on the person's action.

► **EXAMPLE:** Receptionist/polite

person: _A receptionist is polite on the phone._

action: _A receptionist answers the phone politely._

1. Teacher/creative

   person: _____

   action: _____

2. Waitress/quick

   person: _____

   action: _____

3. Nurse/calm

   person: _____

   action: _____

4. Truck driver/careful

   person: _____

   action: _____

5. Mechanic/messy

   person: _____

   action: _____

6. Race car driver/fast

   person: _____

   action: _____

7. Scientist/systematic

   person: _____

   action: _____

8. Pilot/cautious

   person: _____

   action: _____

9. Construction worker/noisy

person: _____

action: _____

10. The president/diplomatic

person: _____

action: _____

▶ **EXERCISE 5**   *(Focus 3, page 194)*

Think of a person, place, action, or thing that fits each category below. Write a sentence using the intensifier *very*.

▶ **EXAMPLE:** a car that goes fast

 <u>A Corvette goes very fast.</u>_____

1. a basketball player who jumps high

_____

2. an athlete who runs well

_____

3. someone in your class who reads quickly

_____

4. a person who works sloppily

_____

5. someone who sings beautifully

_____

6. a plant that grows slowly

_____

7. someone in your class who shops carefully

_____

8. an actress who speaks softly

_____

9. a restaurant where you can buy good food cheaply

_____

10. a writer who writes poetically

_____

11. an animal that runs quickly

_____

Make a group of four students. Compare your answers from Exercise 5 with other group members' answers. Choose the best answer for each category. Share those answers with the rest of the class.

EXERCISES FOR THE TOEFL® TEST

Units 10–12

Choose the *one* word or phrase that best completes each sentence.

1. Kim likes ice cream, but _____ makes her cold.
   (A) she
   (B) it
   (C) he
   (D) you

2. Artie and Gilberto go _____ Los Angeles every year.
   (A) in
   (B) on
   (C) to
   (D) at

3. Monica rushes _____ work every Friday afternoon.
   (A) quickly out of
   (B) quick out of
   (C) quick out at
   (D) quickly out at

4. I need _____ minutes to find my keys.
   (A) little
   (B) a little
   (C) few
   (D) a few

5. The teacher walked _____ the classroom.
   (A) fastly through
   (B) through quietly
   (C) quietly through
   (D) through fastly

6. Drink _____ water instead of _____ cola.
   (A) some glass of . . . one
   (B) a glass of . . . a bottle of
   (C) a can of . . . a glass of
   (D) a . . . a bottle of

7. Betty is very careful with her money; she saves money _____ .
   (A) careful
   (B) carefully
   (C) careless
   (D) carelessly

8. At the grocery store Alice buys _____ .
   (A) a dozen of eggs
   (B) a pound of orange
   (C) a cup of grapes
   (D) a head of lettuce

9. _____ ! That car is out of control!

    (A) Watch out   (C) Put on your blinker when you turn

    (B) Please turn right   (D) Please, try my new car

10. The marathon race goes _____ the center of the city and _____ the bridge.

    (A) through . . . up   (C) through . . . across

    (B) past . . . through   (D) over . . . down

11. The rice is always overcooked. Please _____ .

    (A) watch it carefully   (C) you watch it careful

    (B) it watch carefully   (D) watch you it careful

12. A tornado can blow a roof _____ a house.

    (A) out of   (C) at

    (B) off of   (D) down

13. _____ First Street.

    (A) Turn left on   (C) Turn left into

    (B) You turn   (D) Turn you on

14. There are many fast-food restaurants _____ the highway.

    (A) to   (C) into

    (B) along   (D) out of

15. When the cat and dog need food, I give _____ some.

    (A) it   (C) them

    (B) they   (D) him

Identify the _one_ underlined word or phrase that must be changed for the sentence to be grammatically correct.

16. Enrique has many new books; he reads quick during the winter break.
         A   B   C   D

17. I need to buy a little things at the store.
    A   B   C   D

18. Excuse me, how do I get to the park? Go straight. Walk one block. Then
                       A   B   C

    turn in the corner of Central Avenue.
        D

19. Please has a little more juice. Thanks, it's delicious. Where did you buy it?
           A   B   C

    At the fruit stand.
       D

20. How do I get there? Walk at the corner and turn left.
              A   B   C   D

21. There are few apples in the refrigerator. Please bring me one.
         A   B   C   D

22. After <u>they climb</u> <u>up the mountain</u>, the <u>explorers climb</u> <u>off of the mountain</u>.
 A B C D

23. <u>How much is</u> <u>a box of cereal</u>? <u>I'm not sure</u>. Please <u>to check price</u>.
 A B C D

24. The helicopter always flies <u>up the city</u>. <u>The pilot looks</u> for traffic accidents. He tells the
 A B

drivers <u>on the ground</u> how to get <u>away from traffic jams</u>.
 C D

UNIT 13

DIRECT AND INDIRECT OBJECTS, OBJECT PRONOUNS

► **EXERCISE 1**   *(Focus 1, page 200)*

Underline the direct object in each sentence.

► **EXAMPLE:** Many people play guitars.

1. Other people enjoy guitar music.
2. The guitar has six strings.
3. Each string plays a different note.
4. Guitarists change the notes.
5. They push each string against the neck of the guitar with the fingers of the left hand.
6. This makes the string shorter.
7. The shorter string produces a higher note.
8. Guitarists usually strum the guitar with their right hand.
9. Sometimes they use a pick to pluck the strings.
10. Americans use guitars for many types of music.
11. Acoustic guitars accompany folk music.
12. Rock musicians use electric guitars.

Choose the correct pronouns to complete the story. The first one has been done for you as an example.

Today starts off bad. My dad wakes up late. _____He_____ (He, Him) is in a bad mood, and _____ (he, him) gets a cut while _____ (he, him) is shaving. _____ (He, Him) is grumpy. When my mom gives _____ (he, him) breakfast, _____ (he, him) gets mad at _____ (she, her) This makes my mom angry. _____ (She, Her) yells at my big brother. _____ (She, her) gets mad at _____ (he, him) for no reason. My brother shouts at _____ (I, me). _____ (I, me) feel bad. _____ (I, me) yell at Ruff, my dog. Ruff just looks at _____ (I, me). Ruff barks at _____ (I, me) and gives _____ (I, me) a big kiss. The kiss tickles _____ (I, me).

Read the paragraph, noticing the underlined object pronouns. Draw an arrow from each object pronoun to the noun phrase it refers to and circle the noun phrase. The first one has been done for you as an example.

I don't feel mad at (my family) any more. I want them to feel happy. I have to do something for them. I go outside and pick some beautiful flowers. I give them to my brother, mother, and father. My brother smiles at me. My mother gives me a kiss. I give her a hug. My father smiles at me too. I give

him a hug also. My family is laughing. I really like them when they are happy. Ruff is happy too; my brother is petting him. Ruff finds some milk on the floor and licks it up. When you are happy, everyone is happy with you.

Direct and Indirect Objects, Object Pronouns   **101**

Read the story. For each sentence, write the direct object in the first column and the indirect object that follows in the second column. The first one has been done for you (not all sentences have indirect objects).

Birthday Surprise

► EXAMPLE: Josh plays music for his friends.

1. He sings special songs for his friends.
2. His friends plan a surprise party for Josh.
3. Gwen makes a cake for Josh.
4. Ben buys the decorations for the party.
5. His friends want to buy a special present for him.
6. His friends put their money together for a new guitar.
7. They all give some money to Len.
8. At the music store, Len finds the perfect guitar for Josh.
9. Len gives the gift to Josh.
10. Josh loves the new guitar.
11. Josh sings a special song to his friends.

	DIRECT OBJECT	INDIRECT OBJECT
► EXAMPLE:	music	friends
1.		
2.		
3.		
4.		
5.		
6.		
7.		
8.		
9.		
10.		
11.		

Rewrite the sentences by putting the indirect object before the direct object.

► EXAMPLE: They plan to give a surprise party for Josh.

They plan to give Josh a surprise party.

1. Gwen makes a cake for Josh. _____

_____

2. They all give some money to Len. _____

_____

3. The man hands the new guitar to Len. _____

_____

4. Len gives the guitar to Josh. _____

_____

5. Josh gives his old guitar to Gwen. _____

_____

6. On the weekends, Josh gives guitar lessons to the children in his building. _____

_____

7. He teaches music to the children. _____

_____

8. He also finds used guitars for the children. _____

_____

9. After the lessons, Josh buys sodas for the children. _____

_____

10. In his free time, Josh writes special songs for his friends. _____

_____

At Christmas, Practical Pete gives at least a small present to each of his family members and acquaintances. Use the list of Pete's presents to answer the questions below. The first one has been done for you as an example.

1. Who does Pete give socks to?

Pete gives socks to Brad.

_____

2. What does Pete give the neighbors?

_____

_____

_____

3. Whom does Pete give the hairbrush to?

_____

_____

4. What does Pete give the mail carrier?

_____

_____

5. What does Pete give his girlfriend?

_____

6. Who does Pete give the dictionary to?

_____

7. What does Pete give to his dad?

_____

8. Whom does Pete give the dish towels to?

_____

9. Who does Pete give the car wax to?

_____

10. What does Pete give to his secretary?

_____

11. Who does Pete give the screwdriver set to?

_____

▶ **EXERCISE 7**   *(Focus 5, page 208)*

Pete's gifts are always practical, but they aren't always the best gifts. What gifts do you think would be more appropriate? Write four sentences emphasizing what each person should receive and four sentences emphasizing who should receive each gift.

▶ **EXAMPLE:** _____*Pete gives his mother some perfume.*_____ (emphasis is on what)

WHO

1. _____

2. _____

3. _____

4. _____

WHAT

1. _____

2. _____

3. _____

4. _____

▶ **EXERCISE 8**   *(Focus 6, page 210)*

Change the sentences to pattern B (the indirect object goes before the direct object) if possible.

▶ **EXAMPLE:** Josh says "thank you" to his friend.   *no change*

Pete gives practical presents to his friends and family.

_Pete gives his friends and family practical presents._____

1. I do the homework for my math class every day. _____

_____

2. I hand the homework to my teacher. _____

_____

3. The teacher explains the math problems to the students. _____

_____

4. He teaches algebra to the students. _____

_____

5. He introduces new mathematical concepts to the students. _____

_____

6. He shows the solution to the students. _____

_____

7. Angel offers help to Gretchen. _____

_____

8. He repeats the explanation for Gretchen. _____

_____

9. Angel solves the problem for Gretchen. _____

_____

10. Gretchen corrects her homework for the teacher. _____

_____

UNIT 14

CAN, KNOW HOW TO, BE ABLE TO, AND/BUT/SO/OR

    Mrs. and Mr. Sierra have just bought an apartment building. They want to rent it, but the building needs some repairs first. With the help of their daughter Sisi, they plan to do many of the repairs. However, they must also hire a plumber, a carpenter, and an electrician to help them.

Following is a list of the things they can do and the things they need help with. Write three sentences about each person—one sentence about what he or she *can't* do and two sentences about what he or she *can* do. The first one has been done for you.

MR. SIERRA	MRS. SIERRA
scrape the old paint	paint the walls
repair the window screens	wallpaper the hallway

PLUMBER	CARPENTER
fix the shower	build kitchen cabinets
install a hot-water heater	repair the cracked plaster

ELECTRICIAN	SISI
install a ceiling fan	mow the grass
repair light switches	rake the leaves

MR. SIERRA

1. Mr. Sierra can't fix the shower. _____

2. _____

3. _____

MRS. SIERRA

1. _____

2. _____

3. _____

CARPENTER

1. _____

2. _____

3. _____

SISI

1. _____

2. _____

3. _____

PLUMBER

1. _____

2. _____

3. _____

ELECTRICIAN

1. _____

2. _____

3. _____

▶ **EXERCISE 2**   *(Focus 2, page 220)*

Look at the projects on the list in Exercise 1. With a partner, take turns asking who can do the things on the list. Be honest!

▶ **EXAMPLE: A:** *Can you fix a shower?*
B: *No, I can't. (Yes, I can.)*

▶ **EXERCISE 3**   *(Focus 2, page 220)*

Take a survey: Ask three people if they can do the activities listed below.

	NAME	NAME	NAME
1. speak Cantonese	_____	_____	_____
2. swim	_____	_____	_____
3. drive a car	_____	_____	_____
4. fix a flat tire	_____	_____	_____
5. play a musical instrument	_____	_____	_____
6. cook	_____	_____	_____

Write questions for each of the answers given. Use the underlined words as cues.

► EXAMPLE: <u>When can you visit me?</u>

      I can visit you <u>next week</u>.

1. _____

    You can pick up the papers <u>after 6:00</u>.

2. _____

    You can meet me <u>at the main entrance</u>.

3. _____

    We can rent the TV camera <u>for five hours</u>.

4. _____

    Your father can take the medicine <u>three times a day</u>.

5. _____

    You can find the butter <u>next to the milk</u>.

6. _____

    That's no problem; <u>my dad</u> can show you how to fix it.

7. _____

    We can find the right size <u>at the new mall</u>.

8. _____

    <u>I</u> can drive you to the store.

9. _____

    <u>A good dictionary</u> can help you understand the words better.

10. _____

    You can find the best fruit <u>in the summer</u>.

With a partner, take turns asking whether each of the following statements is correct in English. Correct any mistakes.

▶ **EXAMPLE: A:** Can I say, "My mother can cooks the best chicken and rice" in English?

B: No, you can't. The correct way to say that is, "My mother can cook the best chicken and rice."

1. They can sing very beautiful.

2. I know how to breath.

3. You can speak English very well.

4. You can fishing from this bridge?

5. Do you know how to play a card game?

6. I can no finish in time.

Read the following list. Make a check by each activity that is a learned ability.

___ laughing   ___ reading

___ speaking English   ___ seeing

___ riding a bike   ___ crying

___ hearing   ___ tasting

___ flying an airplane   ___ swimming

___ smelling   ___ writing

Answer the following questions.

1. What is something you know how to do? _____

2. What is something you don't know how to do? _____

3. What is something you can do? _____

4. What is something you cannot do? _____

5. What is something you are able to do? _____

6. What is something you are not able to do? _____

Below is a list of things Ali can and can't do. Write sentences about Ali using *or, so, and,* or *but* as connectors. One has been done for you as an example.

CAN		CAN'T	
swim	ride a sled	dive	drive a snowmobile
float	drive a car	stay underwater	repair the engine
paint	fix a flat tire	a long time	replace a broken
draw	wash clothes	make jewelry	headlight
ice skate	remove stains	make pottery	sew
		ski	iron

1. Ali can swim, but he can't stay underwater a long time. _____

2. _____

3. _____

4. _____

5. _____

6. _____

7. _____

8. _____

9. _____

10. _____

11. _____

12. _____

13. _____

14. _____

15. _____

PRESENT PROGRESSIVE TENSE

Read the story and then complete the sentences that follow with the correct form of the present progressive tense. The first one has been done for you.

I am Jose Villanuevo. This is my family. I have three sisters. Jennifer is my older sister. My two younger sisters, Carmen and Margarita, are twins. I also have a younger brother, Tito, and a baby brother, Ricky. We are on vacation. Right now we are having fun at the Wild Water amusement park.

1. Jennifer ____is looking____ (look) at the lifeguard.

2. Tito _____ (eat) a hot dog.

3. The lifeguard _____ (watch) the swimmers and blowing his whistle.

4. Carmen and Margarita _____ (sit) in the sand.

5. The man _____ (jump) in the water.

6. Mom _____ (buy) the hot dogs and hamburgers.

7. Dad _____ (sleep) on the sand.

8. Ricky _____ (wade).

9. I _____ (slide) down the water slide.

10. The hot dogs _____ (burn).

11. The drinks _____ (spill).

▶ **EXERCISE 2**   *(Focus 1, page 234)*

Rewrite the sentences in Exercise 1 with a time expression at the beginning or end of each sentence. The first one has been done for you as an example.

1. Jennifer is looking at the lifeguard right now. _____

or

At the moment, Jennifer is looking at the lifeguard. _____

2. _____

_____

3. _____

_____

4. _____

_____

5. _____

_____

6. _____

_____

7. _____

_____

8. _____

_____

9. _____

_____

10. _____

_____

11. _____

_____

▶ **EXERCISE 3** *(Focus 1, page 234)*

Work with a partner. Take turns pointing to an activity in the picture in Exercise 1 and, using a contraction, telling each other what's happening.

▶ **EXERCISE 4** *(Focus 2, page 236)*

Look at each of the pictures below and on page 116. Write a sentence describing each activity, using the words in parentheses as cues. Be sure to spell each verb correctly and use the correct form. The first one has been done for you.

1. ____Ricky is wading.____   **2.** _____   **3.** _____

_____   _____   _____

(Ricky/wade)   (Dad/get/sunburn)   (Carmen/dig)

4. _____

_____

_____

(swimmers/splash)

5. _____

_____

_____

(the girls/bury/dad)

6. _____

_____

_____

(hot dogs/burn)

7. _____

_____

_____

(I/slide)

8. _____

_____

_____

(lifeguard/blow/whistle)

TWEET!   TWEET!

9. _____

_____

_____

(Dad/lie in sand)

10. _____

_____

_____

(Mom/buy/food)

11. _____

_____

_____

(Jennifer/smile)

12. _____

_____

_____

(Tito/eat)

Now we're on our way home from the water park. Everyone is hot and tired, and we aren't having fun.

Using the negative form, complete the sentences describing the picture. The first one has been done for you.

1. Tito/feel well _Tito is not feeling well._ _____

   _____

2. The family/have fun _____

   _____

3. Dad/drive carefully _____

   _____

4. Carmen and Margarita/sit still _____

   _____

5. Mom/agree with Dad _____

   _____

6. The air conditioning/work _____

_____

7. I/talk to my family _____

_____

8. Traffic/move _____

_____

9. Jennifer/smile _____

_____

10. Ricky/sleep _____

_____

11. Dad/watch the road _____

_____

▶ **EXERCISE 6**   *(Focus 3, page 238)*

Rewrite the sentences you wrote in Exercise 5 using negative contractions.

▶ EXAMPLE: Tito isn't feeling well. _____

1. _____

2. _____

3. _____

4. _____

5. _____

6. _____

7. _____

8. _____

9. _____

10. _____

11. _____

▶ **EXERCISE 7**   *(Focus 3, page 238)*

Go to a busy place such as a mall or a supermarket and write ten affirmative or negative sentences about things you see people doing.

▶ EXAMPLE: <u>People are carrying shopping bags.</u>

1. _____

2. _____

3. _____

4. _____

5. _____

6. _____

7. _____

8. _____

9. _____

10. _____

Complete each complex sentence below by adding a phrase in the simple present or the present progressive. Use the words provided at the beginning or end of the sentences. Use *but* to connect the two phrases. Be sure to use the correct time expression in your answer. The first one has been done for you as an example.

At Christmas things are different around my house—we don't do the things that we usually do.

1. I usually go to school, <u>but today I'm shoveling snow.</u> (shovel snow)

2. I'm usually in math class right now, _____

   _____ (stay home)

3. (Dad work) _____ today he's putting up the Christmas lights.

4. Mom rarely makes cookies, _____

   _____ (bake)

5. (see boyfriend) _____ now she isn't with him, she's wrapping presents.

6. Ricky usually takes a nap, _____

   _____ (play)

7. (eat fruit) _____ at the moment he's eating cookies.

8. (don't fight) _____, at present they are arguing over a decoration.

9. Mom usually takes care of Ricky during the day, _____

_____ (bake cookies)

10. Dad usually helps me shovel the snow, _____

_____ (put up the Christmas lights)

► **EXERCISE 9**   *(Focus 4, page 240)*

Complete each of the following sentences by telling about an action that is temporary or a situation that is changing in your life. Then share some of the sentences you wrote with your classmates.

1. This week _____

_____

2. Today _____

_____

3. These days _____

_____

4. This month _____

_____

5. Nowadays _____

_____

6. This year _____

_____

► **EXERCISE 10**   *(Focus 5, page 242)*

Read the following sentences. Put both verbs at the end of the sentence in their correct places in the sentence. Be sure to use the correct form of each verb. The first one has been done for you.

1. Dad ____*seems*____ impatient; he ____*is honking*____ the horn. (honk, seem)

2. He _____ the bun, so he _____ the meat. (not eat, prefer)

3. That radio _____ wet; it _____ to me. (get, belong)

4. Mom always _____ where she put her keys; then she _____ for them. (look, forget)

5. I _____ something funny; the hot dogs _____. (burn, smell)

6. I _____ a good job, but I _____ problems with my boss. (have, have)

7. Tito _____ again; that boy _____ food. (love, eat)

8. The water park _____ nice; the kids _____ fun. (seem, have)

9. The car _____ to dad, but he _____ trouble with the air conditioning. (have, belong)

10. They _____ the weather is good; that's why they _____ to the beach. (believe, go)

▶ **EXERCISE 11**   *(Focus 6, page 245)*

Choose an appropriate verb and write a question for each set of words. Ask your partner the questions and record his or her short answers.

▶ **EXAMPLE:** You / other classes

> A: _Are you taking other classes?_____

> B: _Yes, I am._____

1. You / this class _____

_____

2. Your English / better _____

_____

3. You / your classmates _____

_____

4. You / English at home _____

_____

5. You / English grammar _____

_____

6. English grammar / easier _____

_____

7. You / good day _____

_____

8. I / questions correctly _____

_____

9. Your mother / in the United States _____

_____

10. I / clearly _____

_____

▶ **EXERCISE 12**   *(Focus 7, page 247)*

Now, we are getting ready for a big family reunion. There are so many people that Mom made a list of who is coming, what food they are bringing, when they are coming, how they are coming, and where they are sleeping. I hope they bring enough food for Tito!

Look at the lists and write 15 questions about the people coming to the family reunion, using as many different question words as possible. Then answer the questions you write. There are many correct answers to this exercise. Compare your answers to those of your classmates.

▶ **EXAMPLE:** When are Grandma and Grandpa arriving? _____

They are arriving Friday morning. _____

WHO	WHAT	WHEN	HOW	WHERE
Grandma and Grandpa	potato salad	Friday morning	car	twins' room
Uncle Manuel	drinks	Friday 7:00 A.M.	train	living room
Cousin Carla and her husband	fresh fruit	Friday noon	plane	Jose's room
Aunt Luz	cake	Friday evening	car	guest room
Uncle Raul	chips	Friday morning	bus	garage

1. _____

_____

2. _____

_____

3. _____

_____

4. _____

_____

5. _____

_____

6. _____

_____

7. _____

_____

8. _____

_____

9. _____

_____

10. _____

_____

11. _____

_____

12. _____

_____

13. _____

_____

14. _____

_____

15. _____

_____

EXERCISES FOR THE TOEFL® TEST

Units 13–15

Choose the *one* underlined word or phrase that best completes each sentence.

1. _____ a musical instrument?
   - (A) Can you playing
   - (B) Can you play
   - (C) You can to play
   - (D) You play

2. I can sing, but I _____ play a musical instrument.
   - (A) cannot
   - (B) can't
   - (C) no can
   - (D) can

3. Many of my friends play _____ . I like to hear _____ sing.
   - (A) guitar . . . them
   - (B) guitars . . . they
   - (C) guitar . . . they
   - (D) guitars . . . them

4. Do they _____ play other instruments?
   - (A) can
   - (B) cannot
   - (C) know how to
   - (D) can't

5. My friend Simon also _____ the piano.
   - (A) is playing
   - (B) playing
   - (C) plays
   - (D) play

6. He _____ every day. In fact, he _____ right now.
   - (A) is practicing . . . practices
   - (B) practices . . . is practicing
   - (C) practice . . . is practicing
   - (D) practices . . . practicing

7. Where _____ every day?
   - (A) does he practicing
   - (B) he practices
   - (C) does he practice
   - (D) is he practicing

8. He _____ practices at his mother's house.
   - (A) right now
   - (B) at this moment
   - (C) nowadays
   - (D) usually

9. _____ he plays in an elegant bar.
    (A) Now   (C) At this moment
    (B) Tonight   (D) Every weekend

10. Simon _____ to play Spanish guitar music.
    (A) is preferring   (C) prefers
    (B) prefer   (D) is prefers

11. He _____ on some new songs now.
    (A) is working   (C) works
    (B) will work   (D) working

12. Right now he is playing guitar at the bar on the weekends, but he _____ guitar at the bar during the week.
    (A) 's not playing   (C) are not playing
    (B) is playing   (D) plays

13. _____ his job? Yes he _____ .
    (A) Does he enjoy . . . is   (C) Are we enjoying . . . are
    (B) Is he enjoying . . . is   (D) Is he enjoy . . . is

14. His boss pays _____ pretty well.
    (A) he   (C) him
    (B) to him   (D) her

15. That's great—he can enjoy his work _____ a lot of money.
    (A) and make   (C) but can't make
    (B) but can make   (D) and cannot make

Identify the _one_ underlined word or phrase that must be changed for the sentence to be grammatically correct.

16. We're going to the beach. Can Ellen come? Does she can swim?
    A   **B**   **C**   **D**

17. Ellen is afraid of water, but this week we are helping she to swim.
       A   **B**   **C** **D**

18. Where is she taking lessons? At the pool; she is going there every day.
    A   **B**   **C**   **D**

19. Every morning she walks to the pool. She gives to me her towel. Then she puts her toe in
    A   **B**   **C**   **D**
the water.

20. At first she is hating the water, but once she jumps in, she splashes happily.
        A   **B**   **C**   **D**

21. She can no swim perfectly, but she is learning. Now she can swim to her mother.
    A   **B**   **C**   **D**

22. She <u>knows how</u> to breathe. <u>Now</u> she <u>is learning</u> how to breathe when she <u>is swimming</u>.
              A   **B**   **C**   **D**

23. She <u>can go</u> <u>to the beach</u>, but I always watch <u>she</u> carefully.
    A **B**   **C**   **D**

24. She <u>cannot</u> swim well. She <u>needs me</u> near <u>to her</u> when she <u>is swimming</u>.
     A   **B**   **C**   **D**

25. We always <u>stay</u> in shallow water, <u>and</u> we always <u>are watching</u> <u>her</u> and the other little
            A   **B**   **C**   **D**
children.

26. <u>Can</u> your brother <u>makes</u> model airplanes? Yes, <u>this week</u> he <u>is building</u> a new model.
    A   **B**   **C**   **D**

27. He <u>can put</u> the pieces together, <u>and</u> he <u>can't paint</u> the model by himself. He needs
      A   **B**   **C**
<u>me to help him</u>.
   D

28. <u>Who helping</u> <u>him</u> with this model? I <u>am helping</u> <u>him</u>.
    A   **B**   **C**   **D**

29. First, before <u>he builds</u> a model, he <u>reads</u> all the directions. <u>He reads</u> <u>they</u> quickly.
            A   **B**   **C**   **D**

30. Right now <u>I am helping</u> <u>him</u> do the difficult parts. <u>My brother and I</u> like to build <u>them</u>
         A   **B**   **C**   **D**
together.

ADJECTIVE PHRASES

Another, The Other, Other(s), The Other(s), Intensifiers

▶ **EXERCISE 1**   *(Focus 1, page 254)*

Match the following sentences with the pictures they describe. The first one has been done for you.

a

d

e

b

c

1. _d_ The men in the ambulance are paramedics.

2. ___ The boy on the skateboard is going to crash.

3. ___ The man at the traffic light is in a hurry.

4. ___ The minivan on the highway is full of children.

5. ___ The car with the red light on top is a police car.

6. ___ The tricycle with the squeaky wheel belongs to the little girl.

7. ___ The truck parked at the grocery store is full of bread.

8. ___ The fire engine with the ladder is blocking the intersection.

9. ___ The bulldozer with the woman driver is noisy.

10. ___ The car on the country road is a convertible.

11. ___ The elegant lady with the chauffeur owns a limousine.

f

h

i

j

k

EXERCISE 2 *(Focus 1, page 254)*

Circle the adjective phrases in each of the sentences in Exercise 1.

EXERCISE 3 *(Focus 1, page 254)*

Each vehicle on page 130 belongs to one of the people shown on the page. Match each person to the appropriate vehicle. Then write sentences using adjective phrases. The first one has been done for you.

▶ EXAMPLE: The woman with all the children drives the van.

1. _____

2. _____

3. _____

4. _____

5. _____

6. _____

7. _____

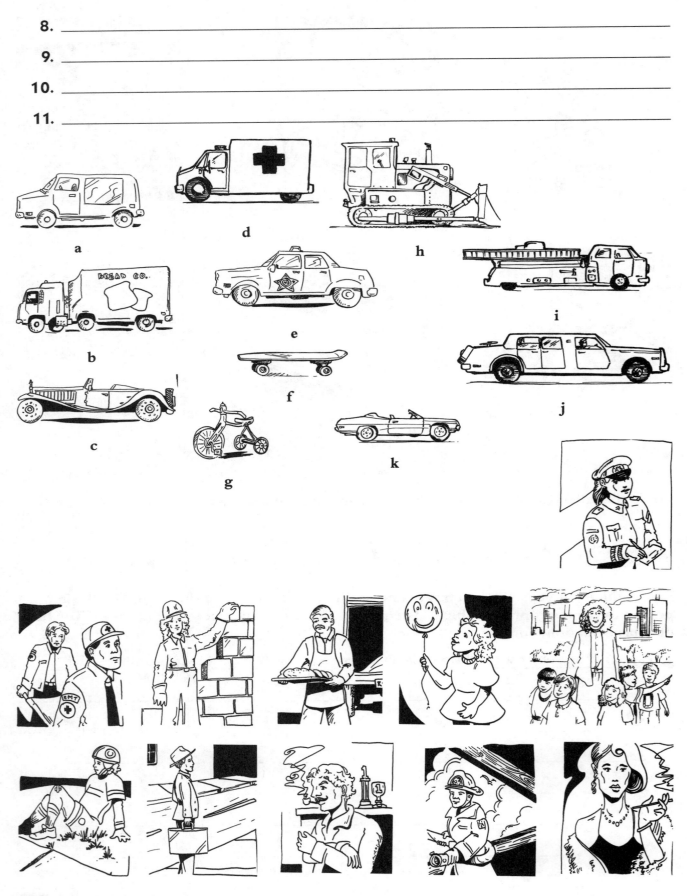

a

d

h

b

e

i

c

f

j

g

k

Cheryl and her daughter Rachel are shopping for school clothes. They each have different ideas about what kind of clothes Rachel should wear. Complete the following by writing *which* questions for each answer.

1. _____

   Cheryl wants to get the long skirt.

2. _____

   Rachel likes the high-heeled shoes.

3. _____

   Rachel prefers long, dangling earrings.

4. _____

   Cheryl wants to buy the pullover sweater.

5. _____

   Rachel likes the skirt with holes.

6. _____

   Cheryl prefers the small earrings.

7. _____

   Rachel likes the tight blouse.

8. _____

   Rachel wants to buy the hooded sweater.

9. _____

   Cheryl wants to buy the flat shoes.

These are the new school clothes Cheryl bought for Rachel. Take turns with a partner asking which clothes they bought.

► EXAMPLE: **A:** *Which earrings did they buy?*
B: *They bought the small ones.*

Complete the following story with *another, the other(s),* or *other(s).* **The first one has been done for you as an example.**

How do astronauts live in space? One problem of living in space is how to keep the astronauts warm. _____*Other*_____ problems are eating, sleeping, and exercising with no gravity. The outside of the space shuttle is covered with small tiles. Under the tiles there are _____ layers of metal to protect the astronauts from the cold of space.

How do the astronauts eat? Some of the food on the space shuttle is in small pieces. The astronauts eat that food through a straw. But they eat _____ foods, such as meat, whole. _____ kind of food they eat whole is fruit. _____ foods that astronauts eat include shrimp, steak, and broccoli. One kind of dessert is candy; _____ dessert is ice cream.

_____ problem for astronauts is sleeping. Some astronauts sleep standing up, while _____ sleep lying down. Astronauts sleep tied to their beds so they don't float around.

While one astronaut sleeps, _____ work or exercise. There are two reasons why the astronauts exercise. One reason is to stay in shape; _____ reason is that their muscles get weak in space.

Think about the following subjects and rate them on the continuum using the adjectives provided. Then write two sentences, one positive and one negative. Use an intensifier in each sentence.

▶ **EXAMPLE:** The English language

difficult .... X .... easy

The English language is fairly easy.

The English language isn't very difficult.

1. algebra
difficult .... easy

_____

_____

2. a Rolls Royce
elegant .... plain

_____

_____

3. horror films
frightening .... funny

_____

_____

4. Antarctica
warm .... cold

_____

_____

5. The Mediterranean Sea
clean .... polluted

_____

_____

6. Moscow

large _____ small

_____

_____

7. airplanes

loud _____ quiet

_____

_____

PAST TENSE OF BE

▶ **EXERCISE 1** *(Focus 1, page 274)*

Match the people and places in the first column with the descriptions in the second column. Then, using that information, write sentences. The first one has been done for you as an example.

1. the Marx Brothers	___	a French general
2. Ernest Hemingway and Mark Twain	___	an Olympic boxer
3. Napoleon Bonaparte	___	African nations
4. Winston Churchill	___	eastern European nations
5. the Soviet Union and East Germany	_1_	a comedy team
6. Eva Peron	___	American rock singers
7. Muhammad Ali	___	a British prime minister
8. Rhodesia and Upper Volta	___	a professional tennis player
9. Arthur Ashe	___	American writers
10. Elvis Presley, Jimi Hendrix, and Jim Morrison	___	the wife of the president of Argentina

1. The Marx Brothers were a comedy team. _____

2. _____

3. _____

4. _____

_____

5. _____

_____

6. _____

_____

7. _____

_____

8. _____

_____

9. _____

_____

10. _____

_____

▶ **EXERCISE 2**   *(Focus 1, page 274)*

Tell your partner three things you felt when you first arrived in the United States or Canada. Then your partner will tell your classmates how you felt. Use the word list to help you.

▶ **EXAMPLE:** You tell your partner:
I was afraid when I first arrived in Canada.

Your partner tells the class:
She was afraid.

WORD LIST

upset	excited	tired	interested	mad	afraid
happy	angry	frightened	nervous	shy	sad

▶ **EXERCISE 3**   *(Focuses 1 and 2, pages 274 and 276)*

Using the cues, write true statements about life 100 years ago.

▶ **EXAMPLE:** expressways: _There weren't any expressways 100 years ago._ _____

1. trains _____

_____

2. horses _____

_____

3. jet airplanes _____

_____

4. skateboards _____

_____

5. United Nations _____

_____

6. a country called China _____

_____

7. two countries on the Korean peninsula _____

_____

8. Olympic Games _____

_____

9. computers _____

_____

10. a prime minister of Canada _____

_____

11. a king or queen of Great Britain _____

_____

12. a president of the United States _____

_____

Find out about your partner. Write questions to ask what he or she was like as child. Check "yes" or "no" depending on his or her answer to each question.

▶ EXAMPLE: <u>Were you friendly when you were a child?</u>

	YES	NO
1. neat	_____	_____
2. helpful	_____	_____
3. happy	_____	_____
4. sad	_____	_____
5. good in school	_____	_____
6. funny	_____	_____
7. messy	_____	_____

1. _____

2. _____

3. _____

4. _____

5. _____

6. _____

7. _____

▶ **EXERCISE 5** *(Focus 4, page 281)*

Write the question for each answer using the underlined words as cues.

▶ EXAMPLE: <u>What was the name of Zimbabwe?</u>

The name of Zimbabwe was <u>Rhodesia</u>.

1. _____

Eva Peron was from <u>Argentina</u>.

2. _____

<u>Mark Twain</u> was the author of *Tom Sawyer*.

3. _____

Muhammad Ali was in the Olympics <u>in 1960</u>.

4. _____

Rhodesia and Upper Volta were <u>African nations</u>.

5. _____

<u>Elvis Presley's</u> house was in Tennessee.

6. _____

Ernest Hemingway was born <u>in 1899</u>.

7. _____

The Soviet Union and East Germany were in <u>eastern Europe</u>.

8. _____

Napoleon was arrested <u>because he supported the French Revolution</u>.

9. _____

Animal Crackers was one of the Marx Brothers' movies.

10. _____

Winston Churchill was prime minister of Great Britain <u>during World War II</u>.

PAST TENSE

▶ **EXERCISE 1**   *(Focus 1, page 288)*

Complete the story with the past-tense form of each verb in parentheses. Check your spelling. The first one has been done for you.

Bernie Bungle _____*tried*_____ (try) to rob the Midnight Market, but Bernie was not a very good robber. This is what happened to him.

Bernie _____ (plan) to rob the store early in the morning, but he overslept, so he _____ (arrive) late.

When he got to the store, he _____ (study) the cashier and customers carefully to make sure there were no police. Then he _____ (cover) his face with a nylon stocking, but the stocking was too thick, so he couldn't see very well. That is why he _____ (trip) when he _____ (enter) the store. All the customers _____ (turn) and _____ (look) at him.

Bernie _____ (point) his gun at the cashier and _____ (demand) all the money. The cashier _____ (fill) a bag with money and _____ (hand) it to Bernie.

After he _____ (rob) the store, Bernie _____ (try) to escape, but the money bag _____ (rip), and some of the money _____ (drop) out of the bag. When Bernie _____ (hop) into his car, he _____ (remember) why he

_____ (want) to rob the store early in the morning. There was a traffic jam, and he couldn't go anywhere.

The police _____ (worry) that the robber would get away. But when they _____ (arrive) at the store, Bernie was only one block away.

► **EXERCISE 2** *(Focus 2, page 291)*

Your teacher will read the following words to you. Listen to the end sound. Put each word in the correct column depending on its end sound.

AT SCHOOL	AT WORK	AT HOME	AT THE PLAYGROUND
learned	walked	vacuumed	played
discussed	delivered	polished	bounced
studied	fixed	ironed	jumped
answered	locked	changed	tripped
listened	worked	cleaned	enjoyed
named	started	baked	climbed
remembered	filed	washed	skated
corrected	pointed	dusted	skipped
printed	typed	brushed	hopped
asked	talked	scrubbed	kissed

GROUP 1 /T/	GROUP 2 /D/	GROUP 3 /ID/
_____	_____	_____
_____	_____	_____
_____	_____	_____
_____	_____	_____
_____	_____	_____
_____	_____	_____
_____	_____	_____
_____	_____	_____
_____	_____	_____
_____	_____	_____

GROUP 1 /T/	GROUP 2 /D/	GROUP 3 /ID/
_____	_____	_____
_____	_____	_____
_____	_____	_____
_____	_____	_____
_____	_____	_____
_____	_____	_____
_____	_____	_____

▶ **EXERCISE 3**   *(Focus 2, page 291)*

With the other members of your group, make a past-tense chain story using one of the groups of verbs on page 141. To make a chain story, one member of the group starts the story. After he or she uses one of the words from the list, the next person in the group continues the story. Each person in the group adds to the story. Make sure that each member of the group pronounces the past-tense verb correctly.

▶ **EXAMPLE: First student:** *When I was in elementary school, I **studied** math.*
   Second student: *I liked math. I **answered** all the questions . . .*
   Third student: *and I always **listened** to the teacher.* (etc.)

▶ **EXERCISE 4**   *(Focus 3, page 294)*

Complete the story with the past-tense form of each verb in parentheses. The first one has been done for you.

As   soon   as   Bernie   Bungle

_____*got*_____ (get) out of jail for

robbing   the   Midnight   Market,   he

_____ (get) in trouble again.

Bernie _____ (see) a house. It

_____ (look) like no one was home. Bernie _____ (break) the window and

_____ (go)   in.   He _____ (look)   for   something   to   steal.   Bernie

_____ (find) some jewelry, and he _____ (put) it into a pillowcase. As he _____ (look) around for something else to steal, he _____ (begin) to feel hungry. So he _____ (take) a look in the kitchen. He _____ (find) a frozen pizza and some beer. Bernie _____ (heat) the pizza and _____ (make) himself some lunch. He _____ (eat) the pizza and _____ (drink) all the beer. Then Bernie _____ (feel) a little tired, so he _____ (sit) down and _____ (fall) asleep. As Bernie _____ (sleep), Mr. Chan _____ (come) home. When he _____ (see) Bernie sleeping in the chair, Mr. Chan _____ (call) the police. Bernie _____ (hear) him and _____ (wake) up. He _____ (stand) up and _____ (run) out of the house. However, the police _____ (catch) Bernie on his way out. Bernie _____ (go) to jail again.

▶ **EXERCISE 5** *(Focus 4, page 298)*

Write a sentence telling what you did at the times or dates given.

▶ **EXAMPLE:** yesterday afternoon

Yesterday afternoon I went out for lunch.

or

I went out for lunch yesterday afternoon.

1. yesterday afternoon

_____

_____

2. last night

_____

_____

3. last weekend

_____

_____

4. six months ago

_____

_____

5. last year

_____

_____

6. the day before yesterday

_____

_____

7. an hour ago

_____

_____

8. last month

_____

_____

▶ **EXERCISE 6**   *(Focus 4, page 298)*

Today is October 31. David Johnson is the gardener at Pine Cone College. He has a busy schedule. The calendar shows what he did in the past month. Write a sentence about the calendar for each of the cues below. The first one has been done for you.

Sunday	Monday	Tuesday	Wednesday	Thursday	Friday	Saturday
29	30	1 *rake leaves*	2 *mow grass*	3 *trim hedges*	4 *fertilize trees*	5
6	7 *trim trees*	8 *rake leaves*	9 *mow grass*	10 *repair sprinklers*	11 *spray for insects*	12
13	14 *repair equipment*	15 *rake leaves*	16 *mow grass*	17 *trim hedges*	18	19
20	21	22 *rake leaves*	23 *mow grass*	24 *plant flowers*	25 *repair sprinklers*	26
27	28 *check tools*	29 *rake leaves*	30 *morning trim hedges* *afternoon mow grass* *night set up president's party*	31	1	2

1. (yesterday)

David trimmed the hedges, mowed the grass, and set up the party yesterday.

or

Yesterday, David trimmed the hedges, mowed the grass, and set up the party.

2. (last week)

_____

_____

3. (two days ago)

_____

_____

4. (on Monday)

_____

_____

5. (yesterday morning)

_____

_____

6. (last night)

_____

_____

7. (the day before yesterday)

_____

_____

8. (two weeks ago)

_____

_____

9. (last Friday)

_____

_____

10. (yesterday afternoon)

_____

_____

Make each of the following statements true by using the negative form in the past tense. The first one has been done for you.

1. Bernie woke up on time on the day he robbed the Midnight Market.

   Bernie didn't wake up on time the day he robbed the Midnight Market.

2. Bernie wore a ski mask on his head.

   _____

3. Bernie got away after he robbed the Midnight Market.

   _____

4. Bernie learned his lesson after robbing the Midnight Market.

   _____

5. Bernie opened the window when he robbed Mr. Chan's house.

   _____

6. Bernie bought some jewelry at the store.

   _____

7. Bernie stole Mr. Chan's TV.

   _____

8. Bernie ate a sandwich.

   _____

9. Bernie drank some coffee.

   _____

10. Bernie slept in a bed.

    _____

11. Mr. Chan called the fire department.

    _____

12. Bernie drove away in his car from Mr. Chan's house.

    _____

13. Bernie escaped from the police two times.

    _____

Can you remember what you did when you were in elementary school? Using the cues, take turns with your partner asking about each other's early school experience. Write down your partner's short answers.

► **EXAMPLE: A:** *Did you wear a uniform to school?*

   B: <u>Yes, I did. (No, I didn't.)</u>

Ask your partner whether he or she

1. wore a uniform to school _____

2. helped the teacher _____

3. studied hard _____

4. rode a bus to school _____

5. got good grades _____

6. sang songs in school _____

7. liked his or her teachers _____

8. played sports _____

9. bought his or her own books _____

10. said "good morning" to the teacher _____

► EXERCISE 9   *(Focus 7, page 305)*

Imagine you are a newspaper reporter. You heard the story about Bernie Bungle, the burglar. You want to ask the victims questions about Bernie's two crimes. Use the question words and cues to write the questions you want to ask. The first one has been done for you.

THE CASHIER AT THE MIDNIGHT MARKET

1. Why / Bernie / trip

   <u>Why did Bernie trip when he entered the store?</u>

2. Where / you / put money

   _____

3. What / happen / to the money

   _____

4. What / police / do

_____

5. Where / police / catch

_____

MR. CHAN

6. What / happen

_____

7. How / he / get in

_____

8. Who / find him

_____

9. Where / you / find him

_____

10. What / you / do

_____

11. How long / he / sleep

_____

EXERCISES FOR THE TOEFL® TEST

Units 16–18

Choose the *one* word or phrase that best completes each sentence.

1. _____ do last night?
   - (A) What you did
   - (B) Did you
   - (C) What did you
   - (D) You did

2. Last night I _____ my mother.
   - (A) visited
   - (B) visit
   - (C) am visiting
   - (D) visits

3. _____ dinner at her house? Yes I did.
   - (A) What did you eat
   - (B) What were you
   - (C) Did you ate
   - (D) Did you eat

4. Yesterday my mother _____ spaghetti for dinner. It _____ delicious.
   - (A) maked . . . were
   - (B) made . . . were
   - (C) makes . . . is
   - (D) made . . . was

5. _____ your mother?
   - (A) Which
   - (B) Which one is
   - (C) Which are
   - (D) Which was

6. The woman _____ my mother.
   - (A) in the polka dot dress is
   - (B) in polka dot dress is
   - (C) with the frying pan works
   - (D) with frying pan is being

7. She's great. Last night she also _____ my clothes, but she _____ them for me.
   - (A) washed . . . ironed
   - (B) washed . . . didn't iron
   - (C) didn't wash . . . didn't iron
   - (D) washed . . . didn't ironed

8. _____ I wasn't living in North America.
   - (A) Three months ago
   - (B) Three last months
   - (C) At three months ago
   - (D) In three months ago

9. Last year I _____ Russia.
  (A) leave   (C) leaved
  (B) am leaving   (D) left

10. The U.S. government _____ me to this country when an American family _____ to sponsor me last winter.
  (A) admited . . . agreeded   (C) admit . . . agree
  (B) admits . . . agrees   (D) admitted . . . agreed

11. The Rosenburg family _____ me money last year.
  (A) sends   (C) sent
  (B) is sending   (D) was

12. When I first _____ to the United States I _____ happy.
  (A) came . . . wasn't   (C) did come . . . were not
  (B) came . . . didn't be   (D) come . . . weren't

13. Mr. Rosenburg, _____ , was very kind to me.
  (A) that man with mustache   (C) that mustache man
  (B) that man with the mustache   (D) that man in the mustache

14. In the beginning, I _____ letters to my family every day.
  (A) write   (C) writed
  (B) wrote   (D) was write

15. _____ problem I had was with the food.
  (A) Other   (C) Others
  (B) Another   (D) Anothers

Identify the *one* underlined word or phrase that must be changed for the sentence to be grammatically correct.

16. <u>What</u> <u>did she</u> <u>taught</u> in grammar class <u>yesterday</u>?
     A   **B**   **C**   **D**

17. <u>What</u> grammar class <u>are you</u> <u>talking</u> about, the morning or the afternoon class? The <u>one</u>
    A   **B**   **C**
  <u>in the morning</u>.
     D

18. <u>Yesterday morning</u> the lesson <u>is</u> easy. We <u>reviewed</u> past-tense verbs and <u>practiced</u> using
        A   **B**   **C**   **D**
  the verbs in sentences.

19. <u>Other</u> grammar class <u>was</u> more difficult. I <u>didn't</u> <u>understand</u> everything.
    A   **B**   **C**   **D**

20. <u>Where</u> <u>were you</u> <u>yesterday</u>? I <u>no see</u> you at school.
    A   **B**   **C**   **D**

21. I <u>was absent</u> because I <u>was</u> <u>very sick</u>. I <u>haved</u> a stomachache.
     A   **B**   **C**   **D**

22. <u>What did make</u> <u>you sick</u>? The <u>night before last</u> I <u>ate</u> something bad and I got food
      A   B   C   D
poisoning.

23. I <u>was</u> so sick, it <u>was</u> terrible. Finally, I <u>told</u> my dad that I <u>wasn't</u> feel well.
    A   B   C   D

24. My doctor <u>wasn't</u> in, so I <u>had</u> to see <u>another</u> doctor. The new doctor <u>in clinic</u> helped me a
            A   B   C   D
lot.

25. I <u>described</u> the problem, and he <u>gave</u> me some medicine. <u>Did the medicine help</u>? <u>Yes, it</u>
    A   B   C   D
<u>didn't</u>.

26. He <u>prescribed</u> two kinds of medicine. <u>One</u> <u>was</u> a pink liquid, and <u>the others</u> was a pill.
      A   B C   D

27. <u>The same thing</u> <u>happened</u> to me <u>last year ago</u>, but I <u>had</u> to go to the hospital.
    A   B   C   D

28. <u>That's</u> terrible! You <u>were</u> really sick. <u>How long you stayed</u> in the hospital? I <u>was</u> there
    A   B   C   D
only one day.

29. <u>The another</u> problem <u>was</u> I <u>didn't know</u> how I was going <u>to pay</u> the hospital bill.
    A   B   C   D

30. My uncle <u>offered</u> to help me. <u>Which uncle is that</u>? My uncle <u>with the big house</u> <u>help</u> me
        A   B   C   D
pay some of the bills.

REFLEXIVE PRONOUNS, RECIPROCAL PRONOUNS: EACH OTHER

► **EXERCISE 1**   *(Focus 1, page 314)*

Write the correct reflexive pronoun in each of the spaces provided in the dialogue. The first one has been done for you.

Paul and Charlotte are having a Halloween party. For the first time, they are putting on a party

all by __themselves__. They are a little nervous.

Charlotte: Are you okay? What happened?

Paul: I'm fine. I just cut _____ a little when I was carving the jack-o'-lantern.

Charlotte: You should wash that cut and get _____ a bandage.

Paul: Okay. Should I put the jack-o'-lantern by the ghost decoration?

Charlotte: No, put it over there alone, by _____. It will look more scary.
How do you like my spider web decorations? I made them all by

_____.

Paul: Great! They look frightening. This is going to be a fun party. I hope the guests

enjoy _____.

Charlotte: I'm sure everyone will have fun. By the way, who's Brad bringing?

Paul: He couldn't find a date. I guess he's coming by _____.

Charlotte: Well, make sure you pay attention to the other guests, too. Sometimes you

and Brad go off by _____.

Paul: Don't worry. I'll spend time with the guests.

Charlotte: Do you think I should pour the drinks now or let the guests help _____?

Paul: Just let them help _____. I hope the guests arrive soon. I don't

want us to have to eat all this food by _____.

Charlotte: They'll be here soon. Oh, we aren't in our costumes yet. We have to get

_____ ready. Will you help me with my costume? I can't zip it up

by _____.

▶ **EXERCISE 2**   *(Focus 2, page 315)*

**Decide whether each of the following blanks requires a
reflexive pronoun. If it does, write the correct pronoun
in the space. If it doesn't, put an X in the space.**

The story continues . . .

Charlotte: I'm all dirty from making those spider webs. First I

think I'll shower _____, and after I dry

_____, you can help me with the zipper.

Paul: Okay. While you're doing that I'll shave _____ and then dress

_____.

Charlotte: What if the guests arrive early?

Paul: We can't blame _____ if they arrive early. I'm sure they can in-

troduce _____. It won't take us long to dress _____.

Later . . .

Paul: See, I told you the guests would enjoy _____. Everyone is

dancing and laughing. It looks like Brad has even found _____

a date. I knew he wouldn't have to be all by _____.

Charlotte: You're right. They are all amusing _____. This is a great costume party. Look at Cindy's costume.

Paul: What is she? She looks like she killed _____.

Charlotte: She's the bride of Frankenstein.

▶ **EXERCISE 3**   *(Focus 2, page 315)*

Discuss the following items with your partner, using reflexive pronouns.

▶ **EXAMPLE:** a holiday your family celebrates without inviting others
      We celebrate Christmas by ourselves.

1. a holiday your family celebrates without inviting others
2. something you want to do by yourself
3. something you can do by yourself
4. something you think a husband or wife can do without his or her spouse
5. a place you do not want to visit alone

Tell the group your partner's answers.

▶ **EXAMPLE:** You say: *I can fix my car by myself.*
      Your partner says: *She can fix her car by herself.*

Match each picture with the sentence that describes it. The first one has been done for you.

1. The children are spraying themselves with water.
2. The children are spraying each other with water.
3. They are spinning themselves around.
4. They are spinning each other around.
5. They're hot. They are fanning themselves.
6. They're hot. They are fanning each other.
7. They are putting makeup on themselves.
8. They are putting makeup on each other.
9. They are washing their faces.
10. They are washing each other.

FUTURE TIME

Will and *Be Going To, May* and *Might*

▶ **EXERCISE 1** *(Focus 1, page 324)*

Clumsy Claire reads her horoscope every day. For the past week her horoscope has come true. Match the picture with the day the prediction appeared. Then match what Claire thought when her horoscope came true. Write it under the picture. The first one has been done for you.

HOROSCOPES

Sunday: You'll get to see nature up close.
Monday: You will buy a new car.
Tuesday: Time will stand still for you.
Wednesday: This will be your lucky day!
Thursday: You will go on a trip.
Friday: A stranger will sweep you off your feet.
Saturday: You'll meet a new love interest.

WHAT CLAIRE THOUGHT

My knee is going to hurt!
I'm going to need a new watch.
He's going to think I'm clumsy.
My car insurance is going to increase.
I'm going to call the exterminator.
I'm going to break my arm.
I'm going to put my lottery ticket in a safe place.

**Tuesday: Time will stand still for you.
I'm going to need a new watch.**

▶ **EXERCISE 2**   *(Focus 1, page 324)*

Read the horoscope section in a newspaper or magazine. Circle the words in the horoscopes that predict future events. Share the horoscopes with your classmates.

Here are some yearbook pictures of seniors at Hilly High School. Read the yearbook captions and then write two predictions of what each person will do in the future. The first one has been done for you as an example.

ALICIA COOPER

Dream
to sing in a rock band
Favorite Activity
playing my guitar

ALBERTA EINSTEIN

Dream
to win the Nobel prize
for science
Favorite Activity
physics experiments

DANA MARINO

Dream
to play football
in the NFL
Favorite Activity
sports

GRACE GUNN

Dream
to own a 1957 Chevy
Favorite Activity
repairing my car

CLARA KLUTZ

Dream
to dance in the New
York City Ballet
Favorite Activity
ballet dancing

ROSS PARROT

Dream
to make a million dollars
Favorite Activity
helping with my
dad's business

CON STRUCTOR	**BRIAN TUMOR**	**CULL T. VATOR**

Dream
to build my own house
Favorite Activity
carpentry

Dream
to find a cure for cancer
Favorite Activity
volunteering at the hospital

Dream
to own my own land
in the country
Favorite Activity
growing plants

Alicia

1. Alicia will meet some other musicians.

2. _____

Alberta

3. _____

4. _____

Dana

5. _____

6. _____

Grace

7. _____

8. _____

Clara

9. _____

10. _____

Ross

11. _____

12. _____

Con

13. _____

14. _____

Brian

15. _____

16. _____

Cull

17. _____

18. _____

▶ **EXERCISE 4**   *(Focus 2, page 325)*

Write the questions for each of the answers given, using the underlined words as cues. The first one has been done for you.

1. Will Ross own oil wells? _____

   <u>Yes</u>, Ross will own oil wells.

2. _____

   Alberta will win the Nobel Prize for science <u>in 2021</u>.

3. _____

   Grace will open her garage <u>in town</u>.

4. _____

   <u>No</u>, Clara will not become rich and famous.

5. _____

   Cull will buy a tractor <u>because it will help him on the farm</u>.

6. _____

   Brian will go to medical school <u>in Boston</u>.

7. _____

   It'll take Con <u>one year</u> to build his new house.

8. _____

   Dana will play football <u>in Miami</u>.

9. _____

   <u>A famous agent</u> will discover Alicia.

Complete the dialogue with the correct form of *be going to.* **The first one has been done for you.**

Helen: <u>Are you going to</u> get ready for the party?

Paul: I don't want to. It _____ be fun at all. This _____ be a boring party.

Helen: It _____ be boring. It _____ be fun.

Paul: Your uncle _____ want to show his vacation slides. The slides

_____ put me to sleep. Then we _____ listen to him talk about

everything in detail. What _____ eat for dinner?

Helen: We _____ have roast beef.

Paul: It _____ be undercooked. I _____ to eat the meat if it is too rare.

Your aunt _____ eat it; then she _____ feel well. I know she

_____ get sick.

Ask your partner to predict the following things. Be sure to use the correct form of *going to* **in your questions and answers.**

▶ **EXAMPLE:** Predict the weather tomorrow.
      A: *What is the weather going to be like tomorrow?*
      B: *It's going to rain.*

1. Predict what grade you are going to get in this class.
2. Predict when the sun is going to set tonight.
3. Predict who is going to be the next person to walk into your classroom.

Look at Suzy's appointment calendar. Today is September first.

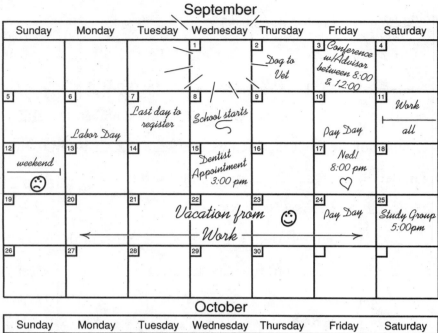

Use the future time expression to tell when Suzy will do each of the following activities. The first one has been done for you.

1. Start school <u>Next week Suzy will start school.</u>

_____

2. Meet with her study group _____

_____

3. Have a dental appointment _____

_____

4. Get paid _____

_____

5. Have a vacation from work _____

_____

6. Have a conference with her advisor _____

_____

7. Have a date with Ned _____

_____

8. Take her first exam _____

_____

9. Have to take her dog to the vet _____

_____

10. Have to work all weekend _____

_____

▶ **EXERCISE 8** *(Focus 4, page 334)*

Look at Suzy's calendar again. Then answer the following questions.

1. What time does the study group meet? _____

_____

2. How long is Suzy's vacation from work? _____

_____

3. What month will she start school? _____

_____

4. What night will she have a date with Ned? _____

_____

5. What time is her dental appointment? _____

_____

6. At what time should she see her advisor? _____

_____

7. How long is it until school begins? _____

_____

8. How long is it until she has to work all weekend? _____

_____

9. What day will she take her dog to the vet? _____

_____

10. Until what day can she register for classes? _____

_____

▶ **EXERCISE 9**   *(Focus 5, page 337)*

Complete the dialogue with the correct form of *will* **or** *going to.*
The first one has been done for you.

Aunt Polly: Tom Sawyer, you ___are going to___ paint the fence.
That is already decided.

Tom: But Aunt Polly, I don't want to paint the fence.

Aunt Polly: I _____ stand for this, Tom. You

_____ cause my death.

You _____ do some work.

Tom: But all the other boys _____ go swimming.

Aunt Polly: Well, you _____ do some painting.

Ben: Why are you carrying that bucket and brush, Tom? What _____ do?

Tom: I _____ paint the fence.

Ben: Why _____ do that? I _____ go swimming. You

_____ have any fun.

Tom: Because I like to. I _____ have fun.
Ben: Hey, that looks like fun, let me try doing it.

Tom: No, Aunt Polly _____ like that. Besides, I'm
having fun.
Ben: Please, Tom, let me do it.

Tom: Okay, but what _____ give me?
Ben: How about this apple?
Tom: Okay.

Read the dialogue again. Write **P** above the answers that predict future events and **I** above the answers that express intentions or prior plans.

▶ **EXERCISE 11** *(Focus 6, page 339)*

What is possible for you in the next year? Write a sentence using affirmative or negative statements and *be going to, will, may,* or *might* to describe your possible future actions.

▶ **EXAMPLE:** get a new pet *I might get a new pet in the next year. (a possibility)*

I'm not going to get a new pet in the next year.

(100% sure that it is not going to happen)

1. get a new pet _____

_____

2. move to a new house or apartment _____

_____

3. finish taking English classes _____

_____

4. win the lottery _____

_____

5. get married _____

_____

6. take a vacation _____

_____

7. read a novel _____

_____

8. get a better job _____

_____

9. be in a car accident _____

_____

10. make a new friend _____

_____

▶ **EXERCISE 12**   *(Focus 6, page 339)*

Share your responses to Exercise 11 with a partner. Explain why you chose "possibility" for some and "certainty" for others.

UNIT 21

PHRASAL VERBS

Read the following story. Circle the phrasal verbs. The first one has been done for you.

My name is Jacques Desire. I am from Haiti. I want to be a journalist, but before I can study my major I have to improve my English.

Today I went to my first college class. I was a little nervous on my way to class. I drove a little too fast. I almost (ran into) another car. I told myself to calm down and slow down. Finally, I made it to class safely.

When I found the right classroom, I saw several students sitting in small groups. "Come in," said one Hispanic woman.

After I sat down, the teacher came in. Immediately I stood up, but I couldn't figure it out. None of the other students stood up. In Haiti we always stand up when the teacher comes into the room. "Please sit down," said the teacher in a kind voice.

Then the teacher handed out some information cards. "Please fill out the card," he said, "and don't forget to write your phone number so I can call you up if I need to."

After we filled the cards out, the teacher handed out an information sheet about the course. He went over the requirements of the class and told us to put the information sheets away in a safe place.

Write captions for the pictures about Jacques Desire's day. Use the following verbs to help you. The first one has been done for you.

hand out	come in	stand up	run into
fill out	go over	calm down	

1.

Jacques almost ran into another car.

2.

3.

4.

5.

6.

Rewrite each of the following sentences two different ways, once with a noun and once with a pronoun. Follow the example.

► **EXAMPLE:** The janitor cleans up the papers.

He cleans the papers up.

He cleans them up.

He takes out the trash.

1. _____

2. _____

He throws away the trash.

3. _____

4. _____

It is time to turn off the TV.

5. _____

6. _____

Please come in. Take off your coat.

7. _____

8. _____

I will hang up your coat.

9. _____

10. _____

**Rewrite the two stories, replacing the underlined words
with phrasal verb s. The first two sentences have been done
for you as an example.**

The house was a mess. Hazel <u>dressed herself with</u> her apron.
First she <u>collected</u> all the trash and <u>put it in the garbage.</u> Then she
<u>collected</u> all the dirty dishes. She <u>cleaned</u> the kitchen. Next she
washed all the family's dirty clothes. She folded them and <u>put the
clothes in their usual place</u>—she <u>placed on a hanger</u> all of the
shirts, blouses, and dresses. Then she vacuumed the rugs. By the
time she <u>pulled the plug on</u> the vacuum cleaner she was
exhausted.

► **EXAMPLE:**   The house was a mess. Hazel put on her apron.

_____

_____

_____

_____

_____

_____

_____

_____

_____

_____

_____

_____

_____

_____

_____

_____

My day started poorly. Last night I forgot to <u>increase the volume on</u> my radio alarm clock. So this morning I <u>opened my eyes after I slept</u> late. I <u>dressed myself quickly in</u> my clothes and ran to catch the bus. I was in such a hurry that I <u>entered</u> the wrong bus. The bus went several blocks before I realized my mistake. I <u>left</u> the bus, and then I tried to <u>solve the problem of</u> how to get to the right bus. Luckily, while I was standing there I <u>met</u> one of my coworkers <u>by chance</u>. He offered to give me ride to work. I gladly accepted. I <u>entered</u> his car. In the end, I got to work on time.

Rewrite the stories from Exercise 4. This time separate the phrasal verbs, if possible.

▶ EXAMPLE: The house was a mess. Hazel put her apron on.

_____

_____

_____

_____

_____

_____

_____

_____

_____

_____

_____

_____

_____

_____

_____

_____

_____

_____

_____

_____

_____

Ask your partner questions about the manners of people in his or her country using phrasal verbs.

► EXAMPLE: men stand when women enter a room

        A: *In your country, do men stand up when women come into a room?*

        B: *Yes, they do.*

1. men stand when women enter a room
2. people usually eat in a restaurant
3. people cross their legs when they sit
4. children do household chores when they get older
5. people usually appear at parties one or two hours late
6. call a repairman when appliances stop working
7. return to the same place for vacation each year
8. knock before they enter a room

Exercises for the TOEFL® Test

Units 19–21

Choose the *one* word or phrase that best completes each sentence.

1. My dog can do many tricks, but there are some things he can't do by _____.
   - (A) itself
   - (B) himself
   - (C) herself
   - (D) myself

2. Are you thirsty? There's some lemonade in the refrigerator. Help _____.
   - (A) myself
   - (B) himself
   - (C) theirselves
   - (D) yourself

3. She fell off the skateboard and hurt _____.
   - (A) by herself
   - (B) by sheself
   - (C) herself
   - (D) sheself

4. Neither boy said who broke the window. They blamed _____.
   - (A) themselves
   - (B) himself
   - (C) each other
   - (D) themself

5. The dance was great. We enjoyed _____.
   - (A) usselves
   - (B) ourselves
   - (C) ourself
   - (D) weself

6. I don't think you can finish that book by yourself. _____ need some help.
   - (A) Will you
   - (B) You're going to
   - (C) You going
   - (D) You are going

7. _____ win the prize for the best actor?
   - (A) Who will
   - (B) Will
   - (C) When will
   - (D) Why you will

8. The almanac predicts that _____ a hurricane in August.
   - (A) there is
   - (B) it will
   - (C) there will be
   - (D) there was

9. What a beautiful morning! I feel great! This _____ a great day!

    (A) is going to be   (C) is going being

    (B) will be   (D) won't be

10. I _____ clean up after you. You must clean your own mess.

    (A) am going to   (C) 'm not going to

    (B) amn't going to   (D) isn't going to

11. _____ study in the library today? No, _____ .

    (A) Are you going to . . . we're   (C) Do you will . . . we won't

        not   (D) Are you going to . . . I am

    (B) Are you going . . . I'm not

12. Don't get too excited. Please _____ .

    (A) calm yourself   (C) calm

    (B) calm down   (D) calm in

13. How _____ to get to Ohio next week?

    (A) he go   (C) does he go

    (B) are he going   (D) is he going

14. _____ we are going to my sister's graduation ceremony.

    (A) Nowadays   (C) A week from today

    (B) Usually   (D) Last week

15. First she will _____ some papers.

    (A) fill in   (C) fill out

    (B) fill   (D) fills

Identify the *one* underlined word or phrase that must be changed for the sentence to be grammatically correct.

16. Will have you time to go shopping for some groceries tomorrow?
       A   **B**   **C**   **D**

17. Will you throw up this trash before you go upstairs?
   A   **B**   **C**   **D**

18. We're going to clean out the town this weekend.
  A   **B**   **C**

19. George is going to hand out the trash bags, and going to get some volunteers.
       A **B**   **C**   **D**

20. Please come in. You can take your coat. I'll hang it up.
      A   **B**   **C** **D**

21. If you fall down , don't worry. Just calm and get up.
       A   **B**   **C**   **D**

22. Be careful! Your going to run into that car.
  A   **B**   **C**   **D**

23. You're going to have to grow up and learn how to put over your clothes by yourself.
     A   **B**   **C**   **D**

24. He's not going to believe this, but I forgot to get up his trash.
     A   **B**   **C**   **D**

25. I won't have any fun this weekend. I'm going go to the beach by myself.
       A   **B**   **C**   **D**

26. What are you going do ? Are you going to write something?
    A   **B**   **C**   **D**

27. No, I'm no going to write; I'm going to draw some pictures.
       A   **B**   **C**   **D**

28. What kind of pictures do you draw? I draw pictures of fruit. Will you draws a picture for
                                                   A   **B**   **C**

me? Sure, I'll get some pencils.
              D

29. What are you going to do this summer? I don't know. I aren't going to go on a vacation.
       A   **B**   **C**   **D**

30. That's too bad! You are going to get a chance to get away on weekends?
       A   **B**   **C**   **D**

COMPARISON WITH ADJECTIVES

Use the following adjectives to compare the shoes of Bob the basketball player and Felicia the fashion model.

comfortable, dressy, expensive, new, old, casual, big

▶ EXAMPLE: Bob's shoes are more comfortable than

Felicia's shoes.

1. _____

_____

2. _____

_____

3. _____

_____

4. _____

_____

5. _____

_____

6. _____

_____

Bob likes comedy movies, and Felicia likes romances. Use the following adjectives to compare the two kinds of movies.

emotional, exciting, sensitive, sad, funny, silly

7. _____

_____

8. _____

_____

9. _____

_____

10. _____

_____

11. _____

_____

12. _____

_____

▶ **EXERCISE 2**   *(Focus 1, page 364)*

My hometown is Skagway, Alaska. It is a small, isolated town—only 500 people live there, but the people are very friendly because they all know each other. The town closest to Skagway is 50 miles away.

Skagway is a historic town. In 1898, Skagway was a gold rush town. At that time, 20,000 people lived there. Most of the buildings from that time are still standing. Every summer thousands of tourists visit Skagway to see both a gold rush town and the spectacular beauty of the surrounding mountains.

In the winter Skagway doesn't have many tourists. It is very cold, wet, snowy, and windy, but in the summer the weather is pleasant. Because Skagway is near the Arctic Circle, the days are long. Sometimes the sun never sets at all.

Using the cues, write sentences comparing your hometown to Skagway.

▶ EXAMPLE: <u>The winter weather in Miami is better than in Skagway.</u>

1. good winter weather _____

_____

2. old _____

_____

3. far _____

_____

4. large _____

_____

5. historic _____

_____

6. touristy _____

_____

7. beautiful _____

_____

8. cold _____

_____

9. wet _____

_____

10. snowy _____

_____

11. windy _____

_____

12. long days _____

_____

13. bad winter weather _____

_____

▶ **EXERCISE 3**   *(Focus 2, page 369)*

Bring pictures of your hometown or city to class. Compare the place you are from with those of your classmates. Tell what you think is better or worse about the place you are from.

▶ **EXERCISE 4**   *(Focus 2, page 369)*

Interview your partner. Ask yes/no questions or *who*, *which*, and *whose* questions. Compare the place your partner is from with the place where he or she lives now. Use the cues to help you.

▶ **EXAMPLE:** **A:** *Which place is more expensive to live in, Guatemala City or New York?*
   B: *New York is more expensive.*
   or
   A: *Is Guatemala City more expensive to live in than New York?*
   B: *No, it isn't.*

1. expensive
2. crowded
3. small
4. bad traffic
5. clean
6. warm
7. beautiful
8. friendly
9. crime
10. interesting

Sheri is from Iran, but she has lived in the United States for two years. Sheri took the personal values inventory, which compares U.S. values with the values of some other countries.

Look at Sheri's responses to the personal values inventory and write sentences expressing similarities and differences. The first one has been done for you.

PERSONAL VALUES INVENTORY

U.S. values		some other countries' values
1. Innovative	X....................................	Traditional
2. Action oriented	.................................·. X	"Being" oriented
3. Individualistic	X	Group oriented
4. Competitive	X	Cooperative
5. Future oriented	X....................................	Past oriented

1. <u>Sheri is as innovative as people from the U.S.</u>

2. _____

3. _____

4. _____

5. _____

COMPARISON WITH ADVERBS

► **EXERCISE 1**   *(Focus 1, page 380)*

What are the differences between boys and girls? Read the questions below. Check the box that shows your opinion for each.

	BOYS	GIRLS
1. Who plays jokes more often?	_____	_____
2. Who works harder?	_____	_____
3. Who studies more seriously?	_____	_____
4. Who listens more carefully?	_____	_____
5. Who gets hurt more often?	_____	_____
6. Who acts more calmly?	_____	_____
7. Who cries more frequently?	_____	_____
8. Who sings more beautifully?	_____	_____
9. Who observes more closely?	_____	_____
10. Who draws more artistically?	_____	_____

► **EXERCISE 2**   *(Focus 1, page 380)*

Using your opinions from Exercise 1, write a sentence for each using the comparative forms of the adverbs.

► EXAMPLE: <u>Girls play jokes more often than boys.</u>

1. _____

2. _____

3. _____

4. _____

5. _____

6. _____

7. _____

8. _____

9. _____

10. _____

▶ **EXERCISE 3**   *(Focus 2, page 382)*

Pia and Dan are twins. Using the cues, write sentences that tell how they are similar or different.

▶ **EXAMPLE:** (draw/creative) <u>Dan draws as creatively as Pia.</u>

1. (spell/good) _____

2. (grow/quick) _____

3. (write/neat) _____

4. (talk/quiet) _____

5. (answer/polite) _____

Nathan and Ned are athletes. Although Nathan has blond hair and Ned has dark hair, they are alike in many ways. Using the cues, write sentences that tell how they are similar or different.

Nathan						
Sunday	Monday	Tuesday	Wednesday	Thursday	Friday	Saturday
31 practice	1 practice	2 practice	3 practice	4 practice	5 practice	6 practice
7 practice	8 practice	9 practice	10 practice	11 practice	12 practice	13 practice

Ned						
Sunday	Monday	Tuesday	Wednesday	Thursday	Friday	Saturday
31	1 practice	2	3 practice	4	5 practice	6
7	8 practice	9	10 practice	11	12 practice	13

6. (jump/high) _____

7. (run/fast) _____

8. (throw/far) _____

9. (practice/frequent) _____

10. (practice/hard) _____

Steve is the owner of Water Trails Kayak Club. Cynthia and her daughter Mariah want to join the kayak club, but first Cynthia has to answer a few questions. Read the information card Steve has to fill out for Cynthia and her daughter and write the questions he asks. The first one has been done for you.

CLUB MEMBER

Name <u>Cynthia Schuemann</u>

Age _____   **1.** *How old are you?*

Swimming ability _____   **2.** How _____

_____

Kayaking ability _____   **3.** How _____

_____

Number of years kayaking_____   **4.** How _____

_____

Frequency of kayaking planned____   **5.** How _____

_____

Distance to kayak_____   **6.** How _____

_____

Distance to kayak club from home   **7.** How _____

_____   _____

Length of Membership:

_____ 6 months _____ 1 year

Method of payment:

_____ check _____ cash

_____ credit card

RELATED FAMILY MEMBER

Name <u>Mariah Schuemann</u> _____

Age _____

Swimming ability _____

Kayaking ability _____

Number of years kayaking _____

Frequency of kayaking planned _____

Distance to kayak _____

8. How _____

_____

9. How _____

_____

10. *How old is your daughter?*

11. How _____

_____

12. How _____

_____

13. How _____

_____

14. How _____

_____

15. How _____

UNIT 24

SUPERLATIVES

How much do you know about Canada? Match the information below.

1. ___ the longest river   **A.** Quebec

2. ___ the tallest mountain   **B.** the prime minister

3. ___ the highest waterfall   **C.** the Milk River

4. ___ the largest lake   **D.** the CN Tower

5. ___ the biggest city   **E.** Mount Logan

6. ___ the tallest building   **F.** Toronto

7. ___ the oldest city   **G.** the United States

8. ___ the highest government official   **H.** Alert, the Northwest Territories

9. ___ the town that is the farthest north   **I.** Lake Superior

10. ___ the earliest European explorer   **J.** Della Falls

11. ___ the biggest trading partner   **K.** Jacques Cartier

Using the information from Exercise 1, write five sentences about Canada.

► **EXAMPLE:** The Milk River is the longest river in Canada.

1. _____

_____

2. _____

_____

3. _____

_____

4. _____

_____

5. _____

_____

► **EXERCISE 3**   (Focuses 1 and 2, page 394 and page 395)

Think of all the people you know who have each of the following characteristics or abilities. Choose the person who is at the top of the group and write a sentence with the correct form of the superlative. Be careful to spell the superlative correctly.

► EXAMPLE: tall _Jim is the tallest in my family._____

writes neatly _Diane writes the most neatly._____

1. silly _____

_____

2. sleepy _____

_____

3. runs fast _____

_____

4. helpful _____

_____

5. sleeps lightly _____

_____

6. pleasant _____

_____

7. heavy _____

_____

8. busy _____

_____

9. sad _____

_____

10. drives slowly _____

_____

11. good musician _____

_____

12. graceful dancer _____

_____

13. has blue eyes _____

_____

14. works hard _____

_____

15. drives far _____

_____

▶ **EXERCISE 4** *(Focuses 1 and 2, page 394 and page 395)*

Repeat Exercise 3, except this time write the sentence about the person at the *bottom* of your lists for the following categories.

1. good writer _____

_____

2. shy _____

_____

3. interesting _____

_____

4. busy _____

_____

5. sings well _____

_____

Use the cues to ask your partner the following questions about his or her country. Answer each other's questions in complete sentences. Record your partner's answers.

► **Example:** famous landmarks

    A: *What is one of the most famous landmarks in your country?*

    B: The Statue of Liberty is one of the most famous landmarks in my country.

1. famous landmarks _____

_____

2. best restaurants _____

_____

3. most interesting sights _____

_____

4. least expensive places to shop _____

_____

5. longest rivers _____

_____

6. most common foods _____

_____

7. biggest industries _____

_____

8. warmest places to visit _____

_____

9. greatest artists or entertainers _____

_____

10. best times to visit _____

_____

11. most beautiful cities _____

_____

Tell the rest of your classmates what you learned about your partner's country. If there are students from the same country as your partner, ask them if they agree with your partner's answers.

▶ **EXAMPLE:** *I learned that one of the longest rivers in Brazil is the Amazon.*

UNIT 25

FACTUAL CONDITIONALS

If

▶ **EXERCISE 1** *(Focus 1, page 408)*

Read the following statements. If the statement is true, write "T". If the statement is false, write "F" and then rewrite the statement to make it true. The first one has been done for you.

1. _F_ If you mix yellow and red, you get green. _____

   If you mix yellow and red, you get orange. _____

2. ___ If you are on the equator, the sun rises and sets at the same time every day. _____

   _____

3. ___ If you don't get enough sleep, you never get sick. _____

   _____

4. ___ If a tadpole grows up, it becomes a butterfly. _____

   _____

5. ___ If you scuba dive underwater, you need an oxygen tank. _____

   _____

6. ___ If there are 366 days in a year, it is a leap year. _____

   _____

7. ___ If you eat too many fatty foods, you lose weight. _____

   _____

8. ___ If your skin is exposed to too much sun, you get a sunburn. _____

   _____

9. ___ If plants don't have sunlight, they grow faster. _____

_____

10. ___ If it is winter, ducks migrate. _____

_____

11. ___ If a surface is smooth, it has less friction than a rough surface. _____

_____

▶ **EXERCISE 2**   *(Focuses 2 and 3, page 409 and 412)*

Tell what you do habitually in the following situations. You may use "when," "whenever," or "if."

▶ **EXAMPLE:** When you want to be alone

If I want to be alone, I go to my bedroom. _____

1. When you want to be alone _____

_____

2. When you need a quiet place to study _____

_____

3. Who takes care of you when you are sick? _____

_____

4. When you want to be with people _____

_____

5. When you are caught in a heavy rain _____

_____

6. When you have too much stress in your life _____

_____

7. When you don't have enough money to buy what you want _____

_____

8. When you don't feel like cooking dinner _____

_____

9. When you have a bad day _____

_____

10. When you get a good grade on a test _____

_____

PART A

Think about when you were a teenager. How did your parents treat you in each of the following situations? Complete the statements.

▶ EXAMPLE: If you came home late

   If I came home late, my parents didn't let me go out again all month. _____

1. If you came home late _____

_____

2. If you got good grades in school _____

_____

3. If you wanted new clothes _____

_____

4. If you didn't clean your room _____

_____

5. If you needed some money _____

_____

6. If you wanted to go on a date _____

_____

PART B

Are you different from your parents? How do you treat your children? (If you don't have children, imagine that you do.)

▶ EXAMPLE: *If my daughter comes home late, I don't let her watch TV.* _____

7. If your son/daughter comes home late _____

_____

8. If your son/daughter gets good grades in school _____

_____

9. If your son/daughter wants new clothes _____

_____

10. If your son/daughter didn't clean his/her room _____

_____

11. If your son/daughter needs money _____

_____

12. If your son/daughter wants to go on a date _____

_____

Exercises for the TOEFL® Test

Units 22–25

Choose the *one* word or phrase that best completes each sentence.

1. _____ take you to drive to work?
   - (A) How does it
   - (B) How long is it
   - (C) How long does it
   - (D) How far does it

2. It depends. If I _____ my house early, it _____ only 30 minutes.
   - (A) leave . . . takes
   - (B) left . . . takes
   - (C) am leaving . . . is taking
   - (D) leave . . . took

3. If I leave my house by 6:00 A.M., the traffic _____ it is later.
   - (A) isn't as slow
   - (B) isn't as slow as
   - (C) is slower as
   - (D) is slowest

4. At 6:00 A.M. I can drive _____ than at 6:30 because there is less traffic.
   - (A) quick
   - (B) quicker
   - (C) more quickly
   - (D) most quickly

5. The early drivers are nice; they _____ the later drivers.
   - (A) are more polite than
   - (B) drive crazy as
   - (C) don't drive crazy
   - (D) aren't driving polite

6. They also drive _____ than the later drivers do.
   - (A) carefulest
   - (B) carefully
   - (C) most carefully
   - (D) more carefully

7. Also, the early drivers don't yell, and they honk their horns _____ .
   - (A) most frequently
   - (B) less frequently
   - (C) frequenter
   - (D) not frequently

8. One of _____ things of all about late drivers is that they don't pay attention.
   - (A) worse
   - (B) the baddest
   - (C) the worst
   - (D) worse than

9. Late drivers put on their make-up or shave while they're driving _____ early drivers.
   (A) more often
   (B) more often than
   (C) the most often
   (D) more than

10. They are _____ drivers of all.
   (A) more dangerous than
   (B) the dangerousest
   (C) the most dangerous
   (D) most dangerous

11. Once I saw a man reading while he was driving. I'm sure he was the _____ driver of all.
   (A) more careful
   (B) least careful
   (C) very careful
   (D) less careful than

12. _____ you have to drive?
   (A) How farther do
   (B) How far
   (C) How farthest do
   (D) How far do

13. It's only 18 miles _____ a shortcut.
   (A) whenever I took
   (B) if I am taking
   (C) if I take
   (D) when taking

14. I know it's the same distance no matter what time I leave, but if I leave later, it seems _____ when I leave early.
   (A) farther than
   (B) the furthest
   (C) farrer than
   (D) far

15. No one at my job travels as far as _____ .
   (A) I can
   (B) I will
   (C) I do
   (D) I am

Identify the *one* underlined word or phrase that must be changed for the sentence to be grammatically correct.

16. <u>Whenever</u> you <u>fly</u> from Europe to <u>North America</u>, you <u>gained</u> time.
      A   **B**   **C**   **D**

17. <u>If</u> it <u>is</u> noon in <u>London</u> , it <u>was</u> 6 A.M. in Montreal.
   A   **B**   **C**   **D**

18. <u>One of the</u> <u>difficultest</u> <u>things</u> about traveling across the Atlantic Ocean <u>is</u> jet lag.
     A   **B**   **C**   **D**

19. <u>The</u> <u>good</u> and <u>fastest</u> way to get over jet lag <u>is</u> to plan ahead.
    A   **B**   **C**   **D**

20. <u>If</u> the time change <u>is</u> <u>more than</u> six hours, your sense of time <u>was</u> distorted.
   A   **B**   **C**   **D**

21. You will do everything <u>very</u> <u>sleepy</u> during the day and feel <u>more</u> <u>alert</u> at night.
                           A   **B**   **C**   **D**

22. The <u>goodest</u> advice I can give you is to make the change <u>as slowly</u> <u>as</u> possible. Don't try
       A   B   C
    to stay awake if you're <u>very</u> sleepy.
                                     D

23. We must <u>treat</u> ocean resources <u>more</u> <u>thoughtfully</u> <u>that</u> we have in the past.
              A   B   C   D

24. Governments need to work <u>more closely</u> with their citizens <u>than</u> they do now. They must
                                  A   B
    preserve marine life <u>more</u> <u>carefullier</u>.
                          C   D

25. Fishermen <u>are</u> <u>worryier</u> <u>than</u> <u>most people</u> about the condition of the ocean.
               A   B   C   D

26. <u>Large groups</u> of fish are <u>least</u> <u>numerous</u> <u>than</u> in the past.
        A   B   C   D

27. Ocean pollution <u>ruins</u> life <u>just</u> <u>as effectively</u> <u>than</u> overfishing.
                 A   B   C   D

28. Oil spills are <u>biger</u> today <u>than in the past</u>; they pollute oceans <u>more frequently</u> <u>than</u>
                  A   B   C   D
    before.

29. Concerned citizens are <u>more aware</u> of the problem. They complain <u>loudly</u> <u>than before</u>
                          A   B   C
    about the problems of <u>the oceans</u>.
                               D

30. They remind us that oceans are <u>just</u> <u>as important today</u> they <u>were</u> <u>in the past</u>.
                                A   B   C   D